Jordan Peterson, God, and Christianity

THE SEARCH FOR A MEANINGFUL LIFE

Jordan Peterson, God, and Christianity

THE SEARCH
FOR A
MEANINGFUL
LIFE

CHRISTOPHER KACZOR & MATTHEW R. PETRUSEK

FOREWORD BY BISHOP ROBERT BARRON

WORD ON FIRE
INSTITUTE

Published by the Word on Fire Institute, an imprint of
Word on Fire, Park Ridge, IL 60068
© 2021 by Word on Fire Catholic Ministries
Printed in the United States of America
All rights reserved.

Design and layout by Cassie Pease, Clare LoCoco, and Rozann Lee.

24 23 22 21   1 2 3 4

ISBN: 978-1-943243-78-5

Library of Congress Control Number: 2020925976

CONTENTS

FOREWORD

In June of 2019, I gave a presentation at the spring meeting of the United States Conference of Catholic Bishops (USCCB) in Baltimore. My topic was what I identified as one of the greatest crises facing the Church today—namely, the massive attrition of our own people, especially the young. After laying out the rather dismal statistics regarding the "nones," or the religiously unaffiliated—50% of millennial Catholics now claim no religious identity, and for every one person who joins the Church, six are leaving—I then shared what I take to be signs of hope, one of which is what I have called "the Jordan Peterson phenomenon."

Peterson's spirited and articulate opposition to the imposition of speech codes in his native Canada made him a controversial political player. He has been seen as a hero of free speech to his supporters and a right-wing ideologue to his detractors. His lectures and presentations, including a fifteen-part series exploring the psychological and archetypal significance of the biblical stories, are avidly watched and commented upon. And his book *12 Rules for Life: An Antidote to Chaos*, which makes for bracing and satisfying reading, is a number one bestseller all over the world, as was his follow-up volume, *Beyond Order: 12 More Rules for Life*. I explicitly told my fellow bishops that my reference to Peterson in no way signaled a one-sided or uncritical endorsement of his teaching. Nevertheless, his emergence and his success are, I argued, indicators that we could get a serious message across to a wide audience. I was drawing my brothers' attention to the rather extraordinary fact that a mild-mannered, soft-spoken psychology professor, speaking of serious matters in a sober way, could attract tens of thousands to arenas and millions to his social media sites.

In many ways, Peterson is doing for this generation what Joseph Campbell did for the previous one: reintroducing the archetypal psychology of C.G. Jung in an appealing and provocative manner. Jung's theorizing centered around what he termed the archetypes of the collective unconscious—which is to say, those primordial instincts, insights, and memories that influence much of our behavior and that substantially inform the religions, philosophies, and rituals of the human race. The Jungian template enables Peterson to interpret many of the classical spiritual texts of Western culture in a fresh way—those very texts so often excoriated by mainstream intellectuals as hopelessly patriarchal, biased, and oppressive. It also permits him to speak with a kind of psychological and spiritual authority to which young people are not accustomed but to which they respond eagerly. He has helped an awful lot of people who have been malformed by a doctrinaire secularism to open their minds and hearts to the truth embedded in the Bible and the great religious traditions.

Despite Peterson's serious engagement with the spiritual life and the history of religion, however, it is not evident that the Canadian believes in God in the accepted sense of the term, a subject we discussed in our first podcast dialogue (see the transcript in the appendix). Instead, Peterson has tended to read the Bible through a Jungian, psychodynamic lens, betraying a Gnostic tendency to read biblical religion purely psychologically and philosophically and not at all historically. No Christian should be surprised that the Scriptures can be profitably read through psychological and philosophical lenses, but at the same time, every Christian has to accept the fact that the God of the Bible is not simply a principle or an abstraction, but rather a living God who acts in history. This living and personal God has remained, for Peterson, an archetype, an idea, a heuristic device. And yet, more recently, Peterson's grappling with the reality of God and, in his own wording, the profoundly "sane" quality of Catholicism, has reached a kind of crescendo in both his life and work.

Whatever the future holds for Jordan Peterson, the book you hold is the first systematic analysis, from a Christian perspective, of both the biblical series on YouTube and his bestselling book *12 Rules for Life*, with an epilogue examining its sequel, *Beyond Order*. Written by Christopher Kaczor and Matthew R. Petrusek, both Fellows of the Word on Fire Institute and both teachers at Loyola Marymount University, *Jordan Peterson, God, and Christianity* offers readers a wonderful summation of the points of contact between Peterson's work and the Christian faith. Although their analysis relies heavily on the insights of Augustine, Aquinas, and the rest of the great Catholic tradition, it largely takes the "mere Christianity" of C.S. Lewis as its point of departure. The result, I hope, is a book that will be of interest, not only to Christians hoping to move beyond all the political rancor and better understand the spiritual and social significance of the Jordan Peterson phenomenon, but also for Peterson fans who are, perhaps for the first time in their lives, thinking seriously about what it might mean to be a Christian.

Bishop Robert Barron

PART I

A Christian Response
to the Biblical Series

Christopher Kaczor

CHAPTER 1

How Peterson Reads the Bible

The most influential biblical interpreter in the world today is not a pastor, a Scripture scholar, or a bishop. He's a Canadian clinical psychologist with no formal training in biblical studies and no church membership.

Jordan B. Peterson's immensely popular YouTube series, *The Psychological Significance of the Biblical Stories* (which has more than eight million views of the first video alone), offers a complex and wide-ranging psychological analysis of the book of Genesis—the stories of creation, Adam and Eve, Cain and Abel, Noah and the flood, the call of Abraham, and more.[1] This series has captured the imagination of committed atheists who rave online about the wisdom Peterson has shown them in the Bible. Countless people, believers and religiously unaffiliated "nones" alike, report that their lives have been changed for the better by this work of explicating some of the oldest stories in human history.

In the first lecture, Peterson acknowledges that his approach to the Scriptures rests on a certain humility before their magnitude and importance:

> I'm approaching this whole scenario, the Biblical stories, as if they're a mystery, fundamentally because they are. There's a lot we don't understand about them. We don't understand how they came about. We don't really understand how they were put together. We don't understand why they

---

1. All quotations from Jordan B. Peterson's Biblical Series are adapted from the transcripts available on his website at https://www.jordanbpeterson.com/category/transcripts/biblical-series/. Future citations will simply refer to the title of the transcribed lecture.

had such an unbelievable impact on civilization. We don't understand how people could have believed them. We don't understand what it means that we don't believe them now, or even what it would mean if we did believe them. On top of all that, there's the additional problem—which isn't specific to me, but is certainly relevant to me—that, no matter how educated you are, you're not educated enough to discuss the psychological significance of the Biblical stories. But I'm going to do my best.[2]

Peterson goes on to lay out his overall approach to Scripture under the following headings: "evolutionary," "psychoanalytic," "literary," "moral," "practical," "rational," and "phenomenological." We might group these under the three broader categories of scientific (evolutionary, rational), literary, and tropological (moral, practical, phenomenological). As we examine each of these categories, what I hope becomes clear is that there is a great deal of overlap between Peterson's approach to Scripture and traditional Christian approaches.

Scientific

In the first lecture, Peterson remarks:

> I'm scientifically minded, and I'm quite a rational person. I like to have an explanation of things that's rational and empirical before I look for any other kind of explanation. I don't want to say that everything that's associated with divinity can be reduced, in some manner, to biology, an evolutionary history, or anything like that. But, insofar as it's possible to do that reduction, I'm going to do that. I'm going to leave the other phenomena floating in the air, because they can't be pinned down. In that category, I would put the category of mystical or religious experience, which we don't understand at all.[3]

---

2. Jordan Peterson, "Biblical Series I: Introduction to the Idea of God."
3. Peterson, "Biblical Series I."

While we will look at the idea of evolution specifically in greater detail in the next chapter, the central point Peterson is making is that his approach to Scripture takes modern science into consideration. Thus one trap Peterson entirely avoids is setting up a fundamental contradiction between Genesis and science. Contra the new atheists, such as Richard Dawkins and Sam Harris, there is no contradiction between science and Christianity. For Peterson, science is telling us what *is* the case, and the text of Genesis is telling us what *ought* to be the case. Genesis encapsulates in narrative form what a successful human being embodies in action. Science is not about action; rather, it is an analysis of what is the case in the material world from a particular point of view. Science is theoretical; the stories of faith are practical.

We can note that there is also a deeper reason for a lack of contradiction between Genesis and contemporary science, and it is tied to the literal meaning of the text of Genesis, which (for the most part) goes unexplored in Peterson's presentation. To properly interpret any text—including the text of Genesis—it is essential to understand the individual context, genre, and style of the text. Even a single word like "Gift" means "a present" in the context of the English language but means "poison" in the context of the German language. The single sentence "I am going to kill you!" is a threat in the context of a heated dispute with an enemy, but a joke in the context of laughing jests with friends. The essential importance of context also pertains to properly understanding what Genesis means.

What does Genesis actually mean on a literal level? By "literal," I mean what the original human author meant to communicate in writing (*ad litteram*) to the original human readers. Only if we properly understand the literal meaning of Genesis can we understand how Genesis relates to contemporary science. Indeed, unless we understand the literal meaning, we might be looking for answers in the text that the text simply cannot provide.

If we were to read the story of Genesis to look for an answer to the question, "Does the text of Genesis support using iPhones or Androids?" we would be asking a question that the text of Genesis does not answer. It is certain that the original author and original audience of Genesis had no opinions whatsoever about contemporary smartphones. Likewise, it is certain that the original author and audience of Genesis had no opinions whatsoever about contemporary science. The author of the Genesis story was neither "pro" nor "con" evolution, and to read the story as taking a stand for or against evolution is to foist contemporary categories and questions on an ancient text. We are free to ask any question we like, including whether the story of Genesis supports using Microsoft. But questions such as these are not useful in understanding the original, literal meaning of the story of Genesis.

C.S. Lewis pointed out that we make a serious error in imposing our own modern distinctions on ancient people:

> What did the early Christians believe? Did they believe that God really has a material palace in the sky and that He received His Son in a decorated state chair placed a little to the right of His own?—or did they not? The answer is that the alternative we are offering them was probably never present to their minds at all. As soon as it was present, we know quite well which side of the fence they came down. As soon as the issue of Anthropomorphism was explicitly before the Church in, I think, the second century, Anthropomorphism was condemned. The Church knew the answer (that God has no body and therefore couldn't sit in a chair) as soon as it knew the question. But till the question was raised, of course, people believed neither the one answer nor the other. There is no more tiresome error in the history of thought than to try to sort our ancestors on to this or that side of a distinction which was not in their minds at all. You are asking a question to which no answer exists.[4]

Inasmuch as the human author and early readers of Genesis did not have the question of evolution in mind, and knew nothing of the debates centuries

---

4. C.S. Lewis, "Is Theology Poetry?" in *The Weight of Glory*, rev. ed., ed. Walter Hooper (New York: Collier Books, 1980), 85–87. This essay was originally read to the Oxford University Socratic Club on November 6, 1944, and published in *The Socratic Digest*, vol. 3, 1945.

Peterson also uses the New Testament to explain and illuminate the Old Testament. In his first biblical lecture, Peterson notes,

> To understand the first part of Genesis I'm going to turn, strangely enough, to something that's actually part of the New Testament. This is a central element of Christianity. It's a very strange idea, and it's going to take a very long time to unpack. This is what John said about Christ. He said, "In the beginning was the Word." That relates back to Genesis 1. "In the beginning was the Word, and Word was with God, and the Word was God."[11]

Augustine also took this approach of interpreting the Old Testament in light of the New Testament, pointing out that the New Testament is concealed in the Old, and the Old Testament is revealed in the New.[12] Likewise, St. Gregory the Great taught that "what the Old Testament promised, the New Testament made visible; what the former announces in a hidden way, the latter openly proclaims as present. Therefore the Old Testament is a prophecy of the New Testament; and the best commentary on the Old Testament is the New Testament."[13] This unity of Scripture is based ultimately on the unity of God and particularly on the work of the eternal Word, operating in creation, in history, and in the texts of Scripture. The medieval master Hugh of Saint Victor notes, "All divine Scripture is one book, and this one book is Christ, speaks of Christ, and finds its fulfilment in Christ."[14]

Peterson's approach of looking to the New Testament to illuminate the Hebrew Scriptures is not at odds but in deep harmony with Peterson's use of any and all available human knowledge to illuminate the text. Pope

---

11. Peterson, "Biblical Series I."

12. In Latin, the phrase is *Novum Testamentum in Vetere latet, Vetus Testamentum in Novo patet.* Augustine, *Quaest. in Hept.* 2.73; see *Dei Verbum*, no. 16, in *The Word on Fire Vatican II Collection* (Park Ridge, IL: Word on Fire Institute, 2021), 31.

13. Gregory the Great, *Homiliae in Ezechielem* 1.6.15, quoted in Pope Benedict XVI, *Verbum Domini*, 41, apostolic exhortation, Vatican website, September 30, 2010, http://www.vatican.va/content/benedict-xvi/en/apost_exhortations/documents/hf_ben-xvi_exh_20100930_verbum-domini.html.

14. Hugh of Saint Victor, *De arca Noe* 2.8, quoted in Benedict XVI, *Verbum Domini*, 39.

Benedict XVI took a similar approach when he said, "To live a faith that comes from the 'Logos,' from creative reason, . . . [is to be] also open to all that is truly rational."[15] If God's reasonable speech gives rise to the created order, and God's reasonable speech gives rise to Scripture, then whatever we learn about the created order can shed light on Scripture, and whatever we find in Scripture can shed light on the created order. God does not contradict God; truth does not contradict truth. In this vision, faith and reason are complementary ways of gaining greater insight on the creation made through God's eternal Word.

Peterson's approach to Scripture is not, at least as far as I can tell, directly influenced by figures like Augustine, Gregory the Great, Hugh of Saint Victor, and Thomas Aquinas. I see no evidence that Peterson is explicitly drawing on any of these figures. Indeed, I've found no reference to these authors—or writers like Jerome, Chrysostom, John Henry Newman, John Paul II, Pope Benedict XVI, or Pope Francis—in Peterson's writings, interviews, or speeches. Noting this absence is not meant as a critique. No one can be an expert in everything. But Peterson reflects the view of Aquinas, who argued that Scripture has an inexhaustible depth of meaning. He rearticulates the view of Augustine, who recommended using all available knowledge, secular or sacred, to illuminate the Bible. And he echoes the view of Hugh of Saint Victor in reading Genesis in light of John's Gospel. Peterson, as it were, reinvents the interpretive wheel that these earlier thinkers had crafted before him, but does so in a way that incorporates contemporary science, literature, and philosophy.

Tropological

Peterson goes on to accentuate a third dimension of his analysis of Scripture, one rooted in the human realities of psychology, morality, and practical action:

---

15. Joseph Ratzinger, "To Be Perfectly Clear," The Catholic Thing, May 13, 2015, https://www.thecatholicthing.org/2015/05/13/to-be-perfectly-clear/.

Morality for me is about action. I'm an existentialist, in some sense, and what that means is that I believe that what people believe to be true is what they act out, not what they say. . . .

The moral interpretation is what to do about what is. That's associated both with security—because you just don't need too much complexity—and also with aim. We're mobile creatures, and we need to know where we're going. All we're ever concerned about, roughly speaking, is where we're going. That's what we need to know: where we are going, what we are doing, and why. That's not the same question as, "What is the world made of, objectively?" It's a different question. It requires different answers. That's the domain of the moral, as far as I'm concerned, which is, "What are you aiming at?" That's the question of the ultimate ideal, in some sense. . . .

Part of the reason that I want to assess these books from a literary, aesthetic, and evolutionary perspective is to extract out something of value that's practical.[16]

In his moral and practical approach to Scripture, Peterson rearticulates, in his unique way, the moral sense of approaching Scripture in Catholicism. From at least the time of Origen of Alexandria in the third century, readers have distinguished various senses of Scripture. In fact, Peterson makes this very point in the third lecture, mentioning Origen by name:

You might not know it, but many of the early Church Fathers—Origen, in particular—stated very clearly that these ancient stories were to be taken as wise metaphors, and not to be taken literally. The idea that the people who established Christianity were all the sort of the people who were Biblical literalists is just absolutely, historically wrong. Some of them were, and some of them still are. That's not the point. The point is that many of them weren't.[17]

---

16. Peterson, "Biblical Series I."
17. Peterson, "Biblical Series III: God and the Hierarchy of Authority."

The literal sense of Scripture is what the human author intended to communicate in a particular genre, such as history, metaphor, poetry, or parable. The allegorical sense is how the passage is related to Christ, the eternal Word and the son of Mary. The moral sense is how the passage can help guide human behavior. And finally, the anagogical sense is how the passage relates to the ultimate human destiny of heaven or hell.

For the most part, Peterson does not attempt to provide the literal meaning of the text. He makes no claim to expertise in the original languages, cultures, or contexts of Scripture. In Peterson's way of putting it, he is looking for the psychological meaning of the text. And the psychological meaning of the text is found in interpretations that help us to live well, to live meaningfully, to bear the suffering of life as best we can. In this focus on action, what Peterson means by the psychological reading of the Bible is what someone like Augustine would call the moral reading of the Bible. In his interpretations of the biblical stories, Peterson shows the enduring power of this classic way of approaching the text, as a source of rich meaning on multiple levels.

In the following three chapters, we will look at Peterson's analysis of the first several Genesis stories, and how that analysis echoes and aligns with influential Christian readings. Then, having explored the points of agreement, in chapter 5 we will explore the question of where Peterson's approach to Scripture could be further developed.

CHAPTER 2

Creation

A Rival Narrative

How can we make sense of Genesis as a contribution to the debates and controversies of its time? If we wish to understand what Genesis means, we must consider the cultural context of Genesis. Peterson takes care to explicate other creation stories circulating in the ancient world, such as the Babylonian creation story, the *Enuma Elish*. In his book *The Lost World of Genesis One: Ancient Cosmology and the Origins Debate*, John H. Walton goes into even greater detail and puts the Genesis story back into its original context so that we can understand better its original, literal meaning.[1] Genesis is written as a reply to *rival stories of creation*.

In the ancient Near Eastern world, other creation narratives asserted that the world as we know it arose from a cosmic battle among the gods. The gods fought violently, tearing each other apart, and the world came to be as a result of this primordial battle. In the Babylonian story of creation, the *Enuma Elish*:

[The god] Marduk defeats [rival god] Quingu and kills [rival god] Tiamat by shooting her with an arrow which splits her in two; from her eyes flow the

---

1. John H. Walton, *The Lost World of Genesis One: Ancient Cosmology and the Origins Debate*. (Downers Grove, IL: InterVarsity Academic, 2009). See, too, Walton's book *The Lost World of Adam and Eve: Genesis 2–3 and the Human Origins Debate* (Downers Grove, IL: InterVarsity Academic, 2015).

waters of the Tigris and Euphrates Rivers. Out of Tiamat's corpse, Marduk creates the heavens and the earth, he appoints gods to various duties and binds Tiamat's eleven creatures to his feet as trophies (to much adulation from the other gods) before setting their images in his new home. . . . After the gods have finished praising him for his great victory and the art of his creation, Marduk consults with the god Ea (the god of wisdom) and decides to create human beings from the remains of whichever of the gods instigated Tiamat to war.[2]

Peterson has talked about this story on many occasions. According to this story, the universe is founded on the chaos of battle, and the rival gods involved in the conflict either emerge from this violence victorious, or their corpses (a disorganized mass of matter) become material for creation.

Genesis proposes a rival story of creation: "In the beginning when God created the heavens and the earth" (Gen. 1:1). Note the striking contrast with the *Enuma Elish*. There is no battle. There is no conflict among rival gods. There is no chaos. There is only calm. And the heavens and the earth do not emerge from the corpse of a rival god. Dennis Prager notes that the word "created" (*bara*) indicates creation from no previous material.[3] Unlike a sculptor who uses preexisting marble to make statue, or a painter who uses brush and canvas to make a painting, God and God alone creates something from nothing, creation *ex nihilo*. Everything in the heavens and on earth has a beginning. In contrast to other stories, only one God brings creation into existence. God creates nature (the heavens and the earth) and preexists nature.

There are two consequences about nature to draw from this first verse. The first is that materialism, the view that nature and nature alone is all that exists, is rejected. Moreover, nature is nonmoral. A fire burns all alike. A hurricane destroys without remorse. If nature alone exists, then the ultimate

---

2. Joshua J. Mark, "Enuma Elish—The Babylonian Epic of Creation—Full Text," Ancient History Encyclopedia, May 4, 2018, https://www.ancient.eu/article/225/enuma-elish---the-babylonian-epic-of-creation---ful/.

3. Dennis Prager, *The Rational Bible: Genesis* (Washington, DC: Regnery Faith, 2019), 2.

reality is not ethical, not loving, and not good. If nature alone exists, then the ultimate reality is blind, pitiless, and amoral. In creating nature (the heavens and the earth), Genesis invokes a divine ultimate reality who (as the story later shows) demonstrates his dominion over nature and his love for human beings.

The second is that nature is not divine; it depends on God.

Nature Is Not God, and God Is Not Nature

Peterson is aware that a fundamental point of Genesis is that nature is not God. He notes,

[God] punishes and rewards, . . . judges and forgives. [God is] not nature. One of the things weird about the Judeo-Christian tradition is that God and nature are not the same thing, at all. Whatever God is, partially manifest in this logos, is something that stands outside of nature.[4]

This is an important idea, a revolutionary idea. In other ancient stories of creation, nature (or at least elements of nature like the sun, moon, and stars) was considered divine. The implications of this idea, that nature is *not* God, would be more fully discovered centuries after Genesis. As Bishop Robert Barron has pointed out, Genesis, in denying divinity to created things, opens the door to the development of science centuries later.[5] If one believes that the sun, the moon, the stars, and the living animals of earth are divine, then the proper response of human beings to the divine is to worship, to adore. But if these realities are created things and not divinities, then it makes sense for human beings to examine them, experiment upon them, and seek to comprehend them. Viewing nature as divine impedes science, and Genesis teaches us that nature is not divine. If nature is not divine, then nature can

---

4. Jordan Peterson, "Biblical Series I: Introduction to the Idea of God."
5. Bishop Robert Barron, "'Cosmos' and One More Telling of the Tired Myth," Word on Fire, March 18, 2014, https://www.wordonfire.org/resources/article/cosmos-and-one-more-telling-of-the-tired-myth/479/.

be dissected, studied, and investigated as an object—that is, nature can be an object of scientific investigation. However, if nature is divine, then nature should be worshiped rather than dissected, contemplated rather than studied, praised rather than interrogated with the scientific method. Early modern scientists did not think of nature as divine because they took seriously Genesis 1:1.

"The earth was without form and void, and darkness was upon the face of the deep; and the Spirit of God was moving over the face of the waters" (Gen. 1:2 RSV-CE). Peterson notes of this verse, "It's hard to get a grip on what 'without form and void' exactly means."[6] The original context of Genesis gives us a clue. There is no structure given to the universe, for it was at this point "without form," and there are no inhabitants, a "void." There are no realms and no rulers. As creation unfolds, God creates various realms, such as the sky and the oceans, to be filled with various rulers, such as the birds of the sky and the fish of the sea.[7] Genesis envisions creation as a massive temple, a house of God, in which various rooms are filled with occupants. But initially, there are no realms and no rulers. How very different is this vision of the cosmos from the crowded battlefield filled with violent agents as in the rival creation stories circulating in the ancient world.

Out of this darkness and emptiness, God brings something new. "Then God said, 'Let there be light'; and there was light" (Gen. 1:3). God creates light not through violent confrontation with rival deities but through rational speech. The universe is brought into being not by a ferocious warrior defeating an enemy but by a spoken eternal Word creating a cosmos. Peterson notes,

> There's this strange idea that Christ [the eternal Word] was the same factor, or force, that God used at the beginning of time to speak habitable order into being.[8]

---

6. Peterson, "Biblical Series II: Genesis 1: Chaos and Order."
7. See Scott Hahn, *A Father Who Keeps His Promises: God's Covenant Love in Scripture* (Cincinnati, OH: Servant Books, 1988), 37–56.
8. Peterson, "Biblical Series II."

By its nature, rational speech is orderly, intelligible, and communicative. To be rational speech, rather than random grunting sounds, appropriate words must be chosen for their meaning, and these words need to be strung together in grammatical sentences and said in the proper order. In contrast, by its nature, a battlefield is disorderly, with parts of weapons here, blood over there, and broken bodies strewn randomly. Genesis proposes to us that the cosmos, unlike a battlefield, is orderly and intelligible. The created order in all its complexity and diversity reflects the orderliness and intelligibility of divine speech, the eternal Word, Christ. We can understand the temporal world because the created order reflects the eternal Word.

Centuries later, the belief in an orderly and intelligible universe led to the development of the scientific method. If seventeenth-century scientists did not believe that the world was intelligible and orderly, they would not have tried to discover the laws of nature. Without belief in an orderly universe, scientific investigation would not have begun. Without the existence of an orderly universe, scientific discovery about the order of the universe would be impossible. Genesis is not contemporary science, but the beliefs of Genesis in an orderly and intelligible universe are presupposed by contemporary science. So we can fortify Peterson's insight that Genesis is not in contradiction to science with an understanding of how the order of nature proposed by Genesis actually leads (centuries later) to science. Though Genesis is not science, early scientists like Nicolaus Copernicus acted on the teaching of Genesis that nature is not divine and that nature is orderly and intelligible.

"And God saw that the light was good; and God separated the light from the darkness. God called the light Day, and the darkness he called Night. And there was evening and there was morning, the first day" (Gen. 1:4–5). God does not obliterate the darkness but adds the light. Our lives on this earth will never be encompassed by pure light, but God enlightens the darkness of our lives partially even here and now. As Peterson notes, the light can be understood as order and the darkness as chaos. Our lives are never pure light, pure order, and hopefully they are also never pure darkness, pure chaos. God names the elements of day and night, exhibiting again the power of rational speech, this time not in creating the world but in categorizing the world. The created order arises from reasonable speech, and reasonable speech also reflects the created order. The Word not only gives rise to creation, but the Word interacts with creation.

The story of Genesis continues as God's divine Speech, the Logos, brings into existence the sun, the moon, the stars, and the living creatures of earth. In contrast to rival stories of ancient times, these things are not portrayed as deities, as gods, but as nondivine creatures. Nature is not divine. Thus, we should not take the amoral actions of nature as our ultimate guide to action.

This includes getting guidance from the stars. One of Peterson's chief inspirations is Carl Jung, who analyzed astrology as a projection of human psychology into the heavens. The enduring religiosity of those who claim no religion is affirmed in the popularity of astrology. It is odd in an age of "science" that the pseudoscience of astrology is still found in magazines and in the imaginations of educated people. Such people say things like, "I'd never date a Leo, because I'm a Gemini." The affirmation of superstitious beliefs points to the enduring relevance of the teaching of Genesis, which teaches that the stars are not divinities guiding our destiny but creations arising from God.

But revelation is not necessary to undermine the reliability of astrological predications. Reason alone is sufficient to debunk astrology. Millions of people share the same birthday—say, August 30—but these individuals do not all share the same personality, fate, or future. Some die young. Some live until ninety-five. Some are healthy, others sick. Some have many friends, some are lonely. Even people born on the very same date—say, August 30, 2000—do not all share the same personality, fate, or future, even though they are born under the same alignment of stars. Even twins born of the same mother, on the same day, and raised under the same roof often have lives that diverge dramatically. The evidence of experience renders the claims of astrology spectacularly stupid. To paraphrase Shakespeare, the determination of fate is not in our stars but in ourselves.

Billions of Years and the Days of Creation

Now, someone like Peterson, who wants to hold together the knowledge of science with the wisdom of the Bible, faces a difficulty. It is important to consider the claim of Genesis that God creates the world in *seven days,* since science indicates that the universe, including the earth, developed over *billions of years.* Surely, someone might say, this timeline inconsistency is an example of faith and reason coming into irrevocable conflict. Seven days is not equivalent to billions of years.

What then can be said about this alleged conflict? In the Bible, the word "day" is not used in a single sense. As Dennis Prager points out:

> "Day" (*yom*) does not always mean "twenty-four hours." In the very next chapter of Genesis, the Torah states, "These are the generations of the heavens and the earth when they were created, *on the day* God made the earth and heavens" (Gen. 2:4—italics added). Clearly "day" in that verse alludes to the entirety of God's creating the world, so in that verse *yom* cannot mean one twenty-four-hour period. "Day" in the Bible means an indefinite period of time just as it can in English, "In that day and age . . ." "in our day . . ." etc. And the Bible itself later asserts, "A thousand years in your sight are like a day that has just gone by, or like a watch in the night" (Ps. 90:40).[9]

Suppose I say, "When I went to high school, social life was different. In my day, no one had a cell phone." No fluent English speaker concludes that I went through high school in twenty-four hours. It would be likewise erroneous to understand "day" in every instance in the Bible as referring to a single twenty-four-hour period of time. Sometimes the word "day" means twenty-four hours, but sometimes the word "day" means just an indeterminate period of time.

---

9. Prager, *The Rational Bible: Genesis*, 19. See also Gen. 2:17.

In the Catholic tradition, the "days" of creation found in Genesis have been interpreted in a wide variety of ways. Some theologians, such as St. Ambrose, did understand the seven days of creation to mean seven twenty-four-hour periods of time. But, for the most part, Catholic readers of Genesis have not understood the "days" of creation as seven twenty-four-hour cycles. Justin Martyr, Irenaeus of Lyons, Cyprian, Clement of Alexandria, Origen, Augustine, Thomas Aquinas, John Henry Newman, Pope St. John Paul II, Pope Benedict XVI, and Pope Francis have interpreted the seven days of Genesis as not related to a twenty-four-hour timeline. [10] Pope St. John Paul II puts the point as follows: "The Bible itself speaks to us of the origin of the universe and its make-up, not in order to provide us with a scientific treatise, but in order to state the correct relationships of man with God and with the universe. Sacred Scripture wishes simply to declare that the world was created by God, and in order to teach this truth it expresses itself in the terms of the cosmology in use at the time of the writer."[11]

Scripture scholar Scott Hahn points out that we might misunderstand the point of the seven days spoken about in Genesis if we do not understand that the ancient Hebrew word for "seven" is the word used for an oath in the context of making a covenant.[12] So when it is said that God created the world in seven days, the text is communicating to its original readers that God has created the world in a covenantal relationship with himself. Genesis proposes not only that the world is an orderly creation from an intelligent God but that God cares about creation. Creation, while not itself divine, is akin to a cosmic temple of the divine, and so should be treated with the respect due to a cosmic temple. In the words of Joseph Ratzinger, the future Pope Benedict XVI, "Creation is oriented to the sabbath which is the sign of the covenant between God and humankind."[13] If this interpretation is correct, then we

---

10. For Pope Benedict XVI's view on this topic prior to his election as pope, see Joseph Ratzinger, *In the Beginning . . . : A Catholic Understanding of the Story of Creation and the Fall*, trans. Boniface Ramsey (Grand Rapids, MI: Eerdmans, 1995).

11. Pope John Paul II, "Cosmology and Fundamental Physics," EWTN, October 3, 1981, https://www.ewtn.com/catholicism/library/cosmology-and-fundamental-physics-8135.

12. Hahn, *A Father Who Keeps His Promises*, 140–151.

13. Ratzinger, *In the Beginning*, 27.

can affirm with Peterson that the wisdom of Genesis and the knowledge of science do not come into fundamental conflict.

Male and Female: Made in God's Image

In addition to debunking astrology and establishing a covenantal view of creation, the text of Genesis proposes this revolutionary belief: "God said, 'Let us make humankind in our image, according to our likeness; and let them have dominion over the fish of the sea, and over the birds of the air, and over the cattle, and over all the wild animals of the earth, and over every creeping thing that creeps upon the earth. So God created humankind in his image, in the image of God he created them; male and female he created them" (Gen. 1:26–27). Peterson glosses this passage: "The two sexes are generated simultaneously, and they both carry within them the divine stamp, which is very egalitarian, very appropriate, and, I think, unbelievably advanced."[14] Because they are both made in the image of God, and God is free, man and woman can also create order from chaos by the free choice of speaking and living the truth. In his second biblical lecture, Peterson notes,

> The notion that every single human being, regardless of their peculiarities, strangenesses, sins, crimes, and all of that, has something divine in them that needs to be regarded with respect, plays an integral role, at least an analogous role, in the creation of habitable order out of chaos—that's a magnificent, remarkable, crazy idea. And yet we developed it, and I do firmly believe that it sits at the base of our legal system.[15]

In some ancient stories of creation, only the family of the king was made in the image of the gods. If you were a crown prince, you were in the divine image, but if you were a commoner, you were not. Genesis is proposing that each person is part of the royal family of those made in God's image.

---

14. Peterson, "Biblical Series II."
15. Peterson, "Biblical Series II."

Everyone counts, men and women alike, a carpenter as much as a king, a penniless peasant as much as a crown prince. In the words of Fr. Richard John Neuhaus, "Nobody is a nobody; nobody is unwanted. All are wanted by God, and therefore to be respected, protected, and cherished by us."[16] This affirmation of universal human dignity led to revolutionary developments later in history. If every human being is made in the divine image, having inherent dignity and value, then all human beings deserve fundamental respect. In later centuries, the respect due to every human being simply in virtue of being a human being came to be called "human rights."

According to Peterson, the story of the first male, Adam, and the first female, Eve, contains enduring wisdom about the human condition. As Peterson puts it,

> I think the reason that the story of Adam and Eve . . . has been immune to being forgotten is because it says things about the nature of the human condition that are always true.[17]

And what precisely are these truths?

The text says, "The LORD God said, 'It is not good that the man should be alone'" (Gen. 2:18). For the first time, something is not good with creation. Family, friends, and (for most people) marriage fit human social needs. As Aristotle put it, man is a social animal. So, God says, "I will make him a helper as his partner" (Gen. 2:18). The literal translation of this verse from the Hebrew is "a helper who is his equal."[18] Prager notes, "The word 'helper' (*ezer*) in no way implies an inferior role. God himself is called *ezer* more than a dozen times in the Hebrew Bible (see, for example, Deut. 33:29, Ps. 121:1–2, and Ps. 33:20)."[19] According to some ancient stories of creation, man and woman don't share equality of the same nature. For example, Plato's *Symposium* contains

---

16. Richard John Neuhaus, "We Shall Not Weary, We Shall Not Rest," *First Things*, July 11, 2008, https://www.firstthings.com/web-exclusives/2008/07/we-shall-not-weary-we-shall-not-rest.

17. Peterson, "Biblical Series II."

18. Prager, *The Rational Bible: Genesis*, 41.

19. Prager, 42.

the speech of Aristophanes in which some protohuman beings arise from the superior sun (the male), others from the earth (the female), and still others from the moon (male-female combination). Even today, some people act as if men are from Mars and women are from Venus. By contrast, Genesis teaches that man and woman share equally in human nature.

Genesis also teaches us something about sexual desire. After finding no animal as a suitable companion, since no animal is equal in nature to a human being, Adam says of Eve, "This *at last* is bone of my bones and flesh of my flesh" (Gen. 2:23; emphasis added). Adam rejoices in the beauty of her bodily presence.[20] In contrast to some ancient stories in which sexual desire is a consequence of divine punishment (see the speech of Aristophanes in Plato's *Symposium*), the original blessing of creation in Genesis includes the sexual attraction of man and woman. The original blessing of creation in Genesis includes God's command to "be fruitful and multiply" (Gen. 1:28). As Augustine notes, "The nuptial blessing, however, whereby the pair, joined in marriage, were to increase and fill the earth, remained in force even when they sinned. Yet it was given before they sinned, for its purpose was to make it clear that the procreation of children is part of the glory of marriage and not the punishment of sin."[21] Sexual desire arises not as punishment from a falling out with God but as part of the original blessing of creation.

Adam and Eve share flesh and bone, which poetically indicates that neither is "more human" than the other. Augustine writes, "Woman is as much the creation of God as man is. If she was made from the man, this was to show her oneness with him."[22] St. Thomas Aquinas argued that if Eve had been created from the head of Adam, she would have been his commander and superior. If Eve had been created from the foot of Adam, she would have been his slave and servant. But Eve was created from the side of Adam, so that she would be his companion in social union with him.[23] In fact, Aquinas

---

20. On this point, see Leon Kass, *The Beginning of Wisdom: Reading Genesis* (New York: Simon and Schuster, 2003), 98–122.

21. Augustine, *City of God* 14.21, quoted in *Ancient Christian Commentaries on Scripture: Genesis 1–11*, ed. Andrew Louth (Downers Grove, IL: InterVarsity, 2001), 39.

22. Augustine, *City of God* 22.17.

23. Thomas Aquinas, *Summa theologiae* 1.92.3.

considers the marriage of a man and a woman to be an "association of equals" in which "the greatest friendship" is possible.[24] These texts provide some ammunition for folks like Jordan Peterson in his wrangling with various feminist critics.

Moreover, inasmuch as all human beings come from Adam, Genesis teaches the lesson that all human beings are part of one human family. Every single person on earth is a distantly related brother or sister. The kinship in family bonds of all human beings is an idea of profound significance. As the Rev. Dr. Martin Luther King Jr. once said, "We suffer from a kind of poverty of the spirit which stands in glaring contrast to our scientific and technological abundance. We've learned to swim the seas like fish and to fly the air like birds. And yet, we have not learned the simple art of walking the earth as brothers and sisters."[25] The lessons that Genesis can teach us are lessons not yet fully learned.

If I Accept Evolution, Do I Have to Reject Genesis?

With the introduction of human beings into the story, a new question about the compatibility of science and Genesis now arises: "If I accept evolution of species, do I have to reject Genesis?" Jordan Peterson, for one, embraces evolution:

> I think in evolutionary terms. As far as I'm concerned, the cosmos is 15
> billion years old; the world is 4.5 billion years old; there's been life for 3.5
> billion years, and there are creatures that had pretty developed nervous
> systems 300 to 600 million years ago. We were living in trees as small
> mammals 60 million years ago, and we were down on the plains between
> 60 million and 7 million years ago, and that's about when we split from

---

24. Thomas Aquinas, *Summa contra Gentiles* 3.123.4, 6, trans. Vernon J. Bourke, updated by Joseph Kenny, OP (New York: Hanover, 1956), https://isidore.co/aquinas/english/ContraGentiles.htm.

25. Dr. Martin Luther King Jr., "Transcript: Martin Luther King's Speech to NATRA, 1967 (Second Half)," *Blog #42*, September 12, 2015, https://www.rimaregas.com/2015/09/12/transcript-martin-luther-kings-speech-to-natra1967-second-half-racism-on-blog42/.

chimpanzees. Modern human beings seemed to emerge about 150,000 years ago, and civilization emerged pretty much after the ice age—something after 15,000 years ago.[26]

Belief in the evolution of species causes some people to think that the story of Genesis is incompatible with science. If the first man, Adam, is created by God, then all life—including human life—did not evolve over millions of years. If all life evolved over millions of years, then there could not be a first man, Adam, created by God.

Is this a real contradiction between faith and reason or only an apparent contradiction? Peterson, for one, sees no real conflict. The stories of Genesis embody a kind of evolution, for they put in narrative form the lessons learned over hundreds, even thousands, of years. Genesis is not a rival to evolution because Genesis captures in narrative form the lessons that those who survive and propagate themselves must live out, even if they do not explicitly understand what they are living out.

There is another way of coming to the same conclusion as Peterson about the compatibility of Genesis and evolution. Among faithful Catholics, including canonized saints, we have already noted that there is a legitimate pluralism in the interpretation of Scripture. Individual believers and theologians may come to different understandings of particular passages while remaining Catholics in good standing.

According to the teaching of Pope Pius XII, Pope St. John Paul II, and Pope Francis, there is no contradiction in believing both in Genesis and in evolution.[27] Of course, the Catholic Church does not require that Catholics believe in evolution or any other view taught by any given scientist. However,

---

26. Jordan Peterson, "Biblical Series I."

27. Pope Pius XII, *Humani Generis*, encyclical letter, Vatican website, August 12, 1950, http://www.vatican.va/content/pius-xii/en/encyclicals/documents/hf_p-xii_enc_12081950_humani-generis.html; Pope John Paul II, "Truth Cannot Contradict Truth," New Advent, October 22, 1996, https://www.newadvent.org/library/docs_jp02tc.htm; Pope Francis, "Plenary Session of the Pontifical Academy of Sciences: Address of His Holiness Pope Francis on the Occasion of the Inauguration of the Bust in Honour of Pope Benedict XVI," Vatican website, October 27, 2014, http://www.vatican.va/content/francesco/en/speeches/2014/october/documents/papa-francesco_20141027_plenaria-accademia-scienze.html.

if one believes in evolution, then one can also—as did Pope St. John Paul II, Pope Benedict, and Pope Francis—remain a faithful Catholic seeking to understand the truths Genesis has to teach us.

What are these truths? Pope Pius XII taught that Catholics may believe in evolution as a way of accounting for the physical development of human beings provided one believes that the souls of human beings (including the first human being) are given by God.[28]

Science and the Soul

But this teaching about the soul raises yet another question. Doesn't science itself disprove the very notion of a "soul"? If there is no soul, then there is nothing tainted with original sin or actual sin. If there is no soul, then the human person is nothing more than an advanced ape.

The first thing to ask of those who allege that science disproves the soul is this: Which scientific experiment shows that the soul does not exist? What is the scientific evidence that the soul does not exist? There is, in fact, no such scientific experiment or evidence. Denial of the soul is a not a scientific discovery but a philosophical theory. It is not science that denies the soul, but a philosophy called materialism—the theory that matter and matter alone exists. And materialism is not something proven by science but is rather a philosophical theory. Indeed, philosophers like Alvin Plantinga have argued that science and materialism are ultimately irreconcilable.[29]

Peterson speaks about the soul,[30] so he may not be among those who think that science has disproved the existence of the human soul. By "soul," what I mean is the immaterial animating principle of the human body endowed with reason. If we think of the soul in this way, science cannot in

---

28. Pius XII, *Humani Generis*, 36.

29. See Alvin Plantinga, *Where the Conflict Really Lies: Science, Religion, & Naturalism* (New York: Oxford University Press, 2011).

30. See, for example, Peterson's comments about the Sistine Chapel in "Biblical Series II": "There's something in it that everyone needs to see. It's not just beautiful. It's more than beauty. It's that which feeds the soul."

principle disprove the existence of the soul. If something is immaterial, it is not directly detectable by empirical means. But inasmuch as the scientific method concerns itself with what can be empirically verified, the scientific method as such is strictly neutral about the existence of nonmaterial things. As Edward Feser has pointed out, the scientific method is akin to a metal detector, which can determine quite accurately the location of a gold ring that was lost in the sand. But a metal detector of its very nature cannot determine whether there is a diamond lost in the sand, for metal detectors are designed to detect only metal and not diamonds. People using metal detectors as the only source of their knowledge would not be justified in claiming that there are no diamonds, rubies, or emeralds in the sand.[31] So, in a similar way, evolutionary theory—inasmuch as it is empirically justified—cannot take a stand for or against the reality of nonempirical things, such as God or the soul. The scientific method as scientific method is strictly neutral about belief in God or in the soul.

Of course, Catholic belief is not neutral about the existence of God and the soul. Is it reasonable to believe in God and the soul? Other works, such as Edward Feser's *Five Proofs of the Existence of God*, address the question of the reasonableness of belief in God,[32] so I will leave that issue to one side. If we follow Peterson and use reason—not just scientific investigation, which is limited to the empirically verifiable—to investigate whether human beings have souls, what can we find? Is it reasonable to believe that a human being has an immaterial rational soul?

Thomas Aquinas thought that it was.[33] His argument for the existence of a nonmaterial rational soul begins with the reality of human knowledge. When I know something like the nature of H_2O, my knowledge of H_2O transcends my senses. According to what I see with my eyes, the lukewarm liquid of water, the scorching cloud of steam, and the cold hardness of ice

---

31. Edward Feser, *Scholastic Metaphysics: A Contemporary Introduction* (Heusenstamm, Germany: Editiones Scholasticae, 2014), 22–27.

32. See, for example, Edward Feser, *Five Proofs of the Existence of God* (San Francisco: Ignatius Press, 2017).

33. Thomas Aquinas, *Summa contra Gentiles* 2.79.

look like three totally different things. According to what I touch with my hand, water, steam, and ice *feel* like three totally different things. But I can know intellectually that water, steam, and ice are actually the very same thing in different forms. The intellectual knowledge of the mind transcends the material knowledge of the senses.

When I know the nature of H20 as such, there is a unity between what I know and my mind. To know something is to have a unity between the knower and that which is known. But this unity is not a material unity. When I know a feather or an elephant, I am unified with the feather or the elephant, but I do not become materially lighter or heavier. To know water is not to become wet. The unity of knower and known is a nonmaterial unity. But if I were only a material being, I could be united with things in only a material way. Therefore, I must not be a purely material being. There must be some part of me, which Aquinas calls my intellectual soul, which is nonmaterial, and allows me to have knowledge—a nonmaterial unity with things that I know.

Aquinas' next step is to note that two material things cannot produce a nonmaterial, spiritual effect. The bodies of the man and the woman can give rise to another body, but if that body is to be not just material but also nonmaterial (spiritual), then some other power must introduce that spiritual element. This power must be able to make something out of no prior existing material, but the power to create something from nothing (creation *ex nihilo*) belongs to God alone.[34] So, if Aquinas' arguments are right, God infuses the spiritual soul not just into the first man Adam but into every living human being.

The text of Genesis emphasizes the material and spiritual nature of the human person in poetic fashion: "The Lord God formed man of dust from the ground, and breathed into his nostrils the breath of life; and the man became a living being" (Gen. 2:7). This passage indicates that the human person is a combination of matter, the dust from the ground, and spirit, the

---

34. Thomas Aquinas, 2.87.

breath from God. To view the human being as pure spirit, as a kind of angel, is to ignore human mortality and materiality as represented by the dust from the ground. On the other hand, to view the human being as mere matter, as only an animal, is to ignore human knowledge and transcendent freedom, as represented by the breath of God infusing the spiritual soul. The Hebrew for "breath of life," *nishmat charyyim*, is "used only for human beings, not animals."[35] Human beings are not spirit alone. Human beings are not matter alone. We are both. What is true of Adam is true of us all.

The view that the human person is a combination of matter and spirit relates to the debates about free will. Peterson knows "that there are debates about all of these things, and debates about free will, and debates about the nature of consciousness, but I'm trying to take a clear look at how people act, how they want to be treated, and then to trace it back to these old ideas to see if there's some metaphysical connection."[36] The metaphysical connection between free will and these old ideas in the biblical stories is this: if we are just matter, and matter is determined, then we are determined and have no free will. But if we are not just matter, if we have an immaterial soul enabling our freedom of judgment and action, then we have a metaphysical basis for our freedom. Peterson's emphasis on freedom and responsibility implicitly presupposes a metaphysics such as this that makes freedom and responsibility possible.

---

35. Prager, *The Rational Bible: Genesis*, 35.
36. Peterson, "Biblical Series II."

CHAPTER 3

The Fall

The Serpent in the Garden and the Knowledge of Good and Evil

Why is the serpent in the garden? Peterson regularly points out that chaos and order are omnipresent in human experience. Human life is unsustainable in pure chaos, but it is also stifled in pure order. The serpent represents the chaos in the otherwise orderly garden. Even if all the snakes could be banished from the garden, the snake of conflict between humans remains a possibility. And even if inter-human conflict could be eradicated, at least after the fall, the snake within each person remains. Peterson's view of the human person is shaped by Aleksandr Solzhenitsyn's insight that "the line separating good and evil passes not through states, nor between classes, nor between political parties either—but right through every human heart."[1] For this reason, Peterson notes, "a serpent, metaphorically speaking, will inevitably appear."[2] The lesson he draws is that it is better to make one's children strong and competent than to attempt in vain to protect them from all snakes. To protect loved ones from all dangers is to make them like infants, depriving them of what could make them creative and strong.

---

1. Aleksandr Solzhenitsyn, *The Gulag Archipelago*, vol. 3 (New York: Harper Perennial, [1974] 2020), 312.
2. Jordan B. Peterson, *12 Rules for Life: An Antidote to Chaos* (New York: Penguin, 2019), 50.

What does it mean to be creative? As noted earlier, God's creativity is expressed through rationality giving rise to creation. Using reasonable speech (*logos*), God says, "Let there be light," and there was light. If the human person is in the image of God, our human creativity will also be a manifestation of rationality giving rise to something new. But what is this creativity exactly? And what, if anything, are its limitations? Genesis provides some material for constructing an answer.

God alone is creative in the sense of making the universe of time, space, and matter out of nothing. Creation *ex nihilo* exceeds human power. But human beings are creative both in terms of what we make and what we do. In terms of what we make, we create through refashioning what exists into new patterns. Paul McCartney wrote the notes of the scale into the song "Let It Be." Shakespeare penned the letters of the alphabet into the sonnet "Shall I compare thee to a summer's day?" Michelangelo chiseled the marble of Carrara into the sorrowful mother holding the corpse of her son Jesus. Creativity in this sense, Jordan Peterson notes, is unbelievably rare, as few of us sculpt a single statue or fashion moving music or poetry, let alone the kind that lasts "so long as men can breathe, or eyes can see."[3] Human creativity in this sense does not extend to everyone. It is said that an admirer once asked: "Herr Mozart, I am thinking of writing symphonies. Can you give me any suggestions as to how to get started?" The great musician replied, "A symphony is a very complex musical form. Perhaps you should begin with something simpler." The man protested, "But Herr Mozart, you were writing symphonies when you were eight years old." Mozart replied: "Yes, but I never asked anybody how."

We will probably not be the next McCartney, Michelangelo, or Mozart, but in terms of what we do, we are all creative. We fashion our choices, characters, and destinies. Each lie shapes our character, and if we continue to lie, we become a liar. Each theft turns us more into a thief. Each cruel act diminishes our compassion. Oscar Wilde's *The Picture of Dorian Gray* vividly

---

3. William Shakespeare, "Sonnet 18," in *Complete Sonnets and Poems: The Oxford Shakespeare* (Oxford: Oxford World's Classics, 2002), 417.

31

depicts how ugly acts disfigure moral beauty. But when we are open to God's grace, every act of hospitality, every donation given to a good cause, and every truth told in love makes us into someone splendid. Both what we make and what we do change us. In both activities we use our powers of reason and will and so act in the image of God.

Some philosophers believe that human persons also create their own values, their own ethical code. Human creativity, on this view, includes the power to make good and evil. In the words of Peterson:

> Nietzsche's idea was that human beings were going to have to create their own values. He understood that we had bodies, motivations, and emotions. He was a romantic thinker, in some sense, but way ahead of his time. He knew that our capacity to think wasn't some free-floating soul, but was embedded in our physiology, constrained by our emotions, shaped by our motivations, and shaped by our body. He understood that. But he still believed that the only possible way out of the problem would be for human beings themselves to become something akin to God, and to create their own values. He talked about the person who created their own values as the Overman, or the Superman.[4]

There are a few problems, however, with creating an ethical system for oneself as if one were God. Peterson notes,

> That was one part of the Nietzschean philosophy that the Nazis took out of context and used to fuel their superior man ideology. We know what happened with that. That didn't seem to turn out very well.[5]

If right or wrong is merely a matter of creative preference, then on what grounds can we criticize the preferences of a totalitarian dictator? Do we actually think "different strokes for different folks" applies to rapists,

---

4. Jordan Peterson, "Biblical Series I: Introduction to the Idea of God."
5. Peterson, "Biblical Series I."

kidnappers, and serial killers? One might reply that we should be able to create right and wrong for ourselves so long as it does not harm other people. But who defines "harm," and who counts as "other people"? History shows us countless cases of the dehumanization of human beings as not fully "persons," from the *Dred Scott* decision to the crimes of the Nazis. Moreover, why must *my* ethical code include *your* requirement not to harm others?

The temptation to ethical creativity (understood as self-determination of good and evil) is as old as the story of Genesis. The serpent tempts the original parents to eat of the fruit of the tree of the knowledge of good and evil—an attempt to have complete understanding and, therefore, to replace God. If someone says, "I know this land from north to south," this person is claiming to know the totality of the land. To claim to know a subject "from A to Z" is to make a claim to complete knowledge of the subject. To have knowledge from the one extreme of "good" to the other extreme of "evil" is another way of talking about complete knowledge, total knowledge, divine knowledge. But divine knowledge does not simply *recognize* what exists; it *creates* all that exists. God alone has divine knowledge, so to eat from the tree is to attempt to become God.

A question arises: Why did God command the man not to eat from the tree of the knowledge of good and evil? To put the question another way, what is wrong with trying to become God?

Imagine a human being who tried to change herself into a dog. She stops speaking and starts barking. She gives up human food for dog food. She no longer stands up straight but crawls on all fours. Of course, no matter how hard she tries to become a dog, she can never succeed. The other dogs know she's not a dog; even she knows she is not really a dog. But what happens is that she has given up the goods that she would have had in living a human life. In trying to become a canine, she deprives herself of human conversation, human food, and human friends. She can never really become a dog, but she certainly can injure or even destroy herself in the attempt.

Almost no one desires to be a dog, but almost everyone desires to be God. The atheist philosopher Jean-Paul Sartre once said, "Man fundamentally is the desire to be God."[6] Fallen human beings wish to replace God with themselves, to become their own God, so that not God but they themselves have absolute freedom. According to this view, "At the heart of liberty is the right to define one's own concept of existence, of meaning, of the universe, and of the mystery of human life."[7] As Dietrich Bonhoeffer put it, "In becoming like God man has become a god against God."[8]

If it is impossible for a human being to become a canine, it is even more impossible for a human being to become divine. The attempt to be God cannot succeed, for we can never achieve divine wisdom, power, and goodness. A caused and limited creature such as ourselves can never become the uncaused and unlimited Creator. But the attempt to become God can result in the loss of the goods that we could have had in embracing our humanity.

If we attempt to become God, we will lose the good of humility, for we will forget that we are earthen creatures of flesh and blood. If we attempt to become God, we will lose the good of justice, for we will forget to give to God and to our fellow creatures what is their due. If we attempt to become God, we will lose the good of love, for love is based on the reality of the beloved and on the reality of ourselves.[9] If we pretend we are divine, our love for others and for ourselves will be disastrously distorted and disordered. It is no accident that the most evil tyrants of history claimed an absolute power that rightfully belongs to God alone. In acting as if they were God, these tyrants exhibited a devilish cruelty to other human beings. By contrast, as G.K. Chesterton noted, "A great man knows he is not God, and the greater he is the better he knows it."[10]

Another question arises: Why did God give them the possibility of eating of the fruit of the tree of the knowledge of good and evil? Why did God give

---

6. Jean-Paul Sartre, *Existentialism and Human Emotions* (New York: Citadel, 1985), 63.

7. *Casey v. Planned Parenthood of Southeastern Pennsylvania*, 505 US 833, no. 851.

8. Dietrich Bonhoeffer, *Ethics* (New York: Touchstone, 1955), 23.

9. Alexander Pruss, *One Body: An Essay in Christian Sexual Ethics* (Notre Dame, IN: University of Notre Dame Press, 2013), chap. 2.

10. G.K. Chesterton, *The Everlasting Man* (San Francisco: Ignatius Press, 1993), 204.

them freedom? Why didn't God choose to reign over a kingdom of chemicals in perfect order and complete lack of freedom?

We cannot have love unless we have freedom. And if we are free to live in the truth of our humanity and the truth about divinity, then we here below also have the freedom to not live in this truth. God could have ruled over a kingdom of chemicals, but God wanted a universe in which love was diffused throughout, and if there is to be love, there must be freedom. According to Genesis, the first woman and the first man misuse this freedom, as do, at least sometimes, every woman and every man now on planet Earth.

"Now the serpent was more crafty than any other wild animal that the LORD God had made. He said to the woman, "Did God say, 'You shall not eat from any tree in the garden'?" (Gen. 3:1). Notice how the serpent distorts the original command. God said, "You may freely eat of *every tree* of the garden; but of the tree of the knowledge of good and evil you shall not eat" (Gen. 2:17; emphasis added). Satan's question makes it sound like God commanded them not to eat of *any tree.* Satan is planting a seed of doubt about God's wisdom and goodness, making it seem like God unreasonably limited their freedom, took away their freedom to eat of any tree in the garden. God, in other words, is a rival.

Eve then responds to the serpent, "We may eat of the fruit of the trees in the garden; but God said, 'You shall not eat of the fruit of the tree that is in the middle of the garden, nor shall you touch it, or you shall die'" (Gen. 3:2–3). Perhaps the distortions of Satan are having their effect, for here the woman also distorts the command of God, adding a restriction, "nor shall you touch it," that was not in the original command. It is as if the woman is saying to the serpent, "Yes, you have a point about God's unreasonable commands."

The serpent promises that Eve will attain to divinity in having complete knowledge from one extreme to the other, knowing good and evil. In the words of St. John Chrysostom, the serpent "caused her to set her thoughts on goals beyond her real capabilities, in order that she might be puffed up with empty hopes and lose her hold on the advantages already accorded her."[11]

11. John Chrysostom, *Homilies on Genesis* 16.11, quoted in *Ancient Christian Commentaries on Scripture: Genesis 1–11*, ed. Andrew Louth (Downers Grove, IL: InterVarsity, 2001), 77.

Rather than humbly accepting inherent human limitations in knowledge and freedom, the serpent tempts Eve to a pride that refuses limitations and seeks to become divine. The serpent tempts: do not accept your humanity with humility, but in your pride become divine. "By pride," writes Augustine of Adam and Eve, "they imagined that they were themselves the source of their being. . . . Whoever seeks to be more than he is becomes less. Whenever he aspires to be self-sufficing, he retreats from the One who is truly sufficient for him."[12] The first sin of Adam and Eve is the prototype of sin in every age, in every human heart: the denial of creaturely nature and the desire to be God. Unlike proper humility, a vicious pride refuses to acknowledge limits and imperfections.[13] As Peterson puts it, "I think the reason that the story of Adam and Eve . . . has been immune to being forgotten is because it says things about the nature of the human condition that are always true."[14] The story of Adam and Eve is the story of Everyman and Everywoman, the story of you and of me.

The Fall and Its Consequences

Eve capitulates to the serpent: "So when the woman saw that the tree was good for food, and that it was a delight to the eyes, and that the tree was to be desired to make one wise, she took of its fruit and ate" (Gen. 3:6). The fruit of the tree looked good for food, delighting the eyes. By this fruit, she could also gain divine wisdom, becoming like God herself. The temptation, therefore, was great. It appealed to the eyes as something that would be tasty and give pleasure. It appealed to the ego as something that would enhance humanity. She gave in.

Then, "she also gave some to her husband, who was with her, and he ate" (Gen. 3:6). This passage gives rise to another question. Who is more to

---

12. Augustine, *City of God* 14.13, quoted in *Ancient Christian Commentaries on Scripture: Genesis 1–11*, 77.

13. On humility and pride, see Dennis Whitcomb, Heather Battaly, Jason Baehr, and Daniel Howard-Snyder, "Intellectual Humility: Owning Our Limitations," *Philosophy and Phenomenological Research* 94, no. 3 (2017): 509–539, https://onlinelibrary.wiley.com/doi/abs/10.1111/phpr.12228.

14. Peterson, "Biblical Series II: Genesis 1: Chaos and Order."

blame, Adam or Eve? Some interpreters view Eve as more to blame and use this interpretation as evidence of an anti-female bias in the text. Peterson notes,

> There's a modern feminist interpretation of the story of Adam and Eve that makes the claim that Eve was portrayed as the universal bad guy of humanity for disobeying God and eating the apple. . . . It looks like she slipped up, and then she tempted her husband, and that makes her even worse—although, he was foolish enough to immediately eat, so it just means that she was a little more courageous than him and got there first.[15]

Ambrose of Milan suggests another interpretation. Ambrose notes that God directly commanded Adam not to eat of the fruit, and that there is no indication that God directly commanded Eve, who learned of this command by means of Adam.[16] But it is worse to disobey a command directly given by God than to disobey a command not directly given by God. If a police officer tells you, "Move your car," and you don't move it, that seems worse than if your friend says, "The cop said to move your car," and you don't move it. Adam directly disobeyed God; Eve did not.

Moreover, Eve is not the "weak link" in comparison to Adam. As St. Irenaeus wrote centuries ago:

> Why did the serpent not attack the man, rather than the woman? You say he went after her because she was the weaker of the two. On the contrary. In the transgression of the commandment, she showed herself to be the stronger. . . . For she alone stood up to the serpent. She ate from the tree, but with resistance and dissent and after being dealt with perfidiously. But Adam partook of the fruit given by the woman, without even beginning to make a fight, without a word of contradiction—a perfect demonstration of

---

15. Peterson, "Biblical Series IV: Adam and Eve: Self-Consciousness, Evil, and Death."
16. Ambrose, *Paradise* 12, quoted in *Ancient Christian Commentaries on Scripture: Genesis 1–11*, 76.

consummate weakness and a cowardly soul. The woman, moreover, can be excluded; she wrestled with a demon and was thrown. But Adam will not be able to find an excuse.[17]

Eve resisted the temptation; Adam did not. If two people do the same action, but one reluctantly and only after pressure gives in, that person seems to have done better than the person who does what is wrong without any resistance. In any case, they both capitulated in the end.

"Then the eyes of both were opened, and they knew that they were naked; and they sewed fig leaves together and made loincloths for themselves" (Gen. 3:7). This verse cannot mean that their eyes were physically shut or that they were blind before eating the fruit. The immediately previous verse indicates that "the woman saw that the tree was good for food" (Gen. 3:6). In naming the animals, Adam presumably first saw each one so as to be able to categorize them. Adam saw and appreciated Eve's beauty. Peterson interprets this verse to mean that the eyes of both are opened in that they become self-conscious. Once they eat the fruit, Adam and Eve realize that they are naked, unprotected, and vulnerable. They realize how they can be hurt, how they will die, and how anyone like them is also vulnerable to death and suffering. With awareness of human vulnerability, the human choice of malevolence becomes possible. Mere animals also die, but they lack the self-consciousness to project their own mortality into the future. Mere animals kill, but the malevolence of the sons of Adam, Cain against Abel, is a possibility only for humankind.

After the sin comes the reckoning for sin: "They heard the sound of the LORD God walking in the garden at the time of the evening breeze, and the man and his wife hid themselves from the presence of the LORD God among the trees of the garden. But the LORD God called to the man, and said to him, 'Where are you?'" (Gen. 3:8–10). To sin is to act against love, and love is partially constituted by the desire for unity with the beloved.[18] So when Adam and

---

17. Irenaeus, *Against Heresies* 1.10.3, quoted in Scott Hahn, *A Father Who Keeps His Promises: God's Covenant Love in Scripture* (Cincinnati, OH: Servant Books, 1998), 65.

18. Pruss, *One Body*, chap. 2.

Eve sin, they seek not greater unity with God and with each other; rather, they seek to hide from God and conceal themselves in clothing from each other. The original couple goes from trying to become God to hiding from God.

If God is all knowing, why would he call to the man and ask, "Where are you?" The question is not about his location in the garden. If, as the text of Genesis teaches, God creates and governs the entire universe—all space, time, and matter—then obviously God's power and omniscience extends to knowing the location of Adam. Peterson sees this question as a bit of comic relief to ease the tension of the drama: "I love this part of the story. It's so funny, and we could use a little humor at this point."[19]

I wonder, though, if the real point of God's question is not comedy but confession. After their sin, God shows his loving-kindness by inviting them to self-reflection and honesty. St. John Chrysostom writes that God "asks a question, receives a reply and questions them further as if inviting them to excuse themselves so that he might seize the opportunity to display his characteristic love in regard to the sinners, even despite their fall."[20] In this part of the story, God is akin to a mother who sees her three-year-old son with chocolate cookie crumbs all over his face and says, "Did you get into the cookies that I told you not to eat?" She knows, of course, that he did. She asks him the question not in order to gain knowledge that she lacks but in order to elicit from him an honest apology. He damaged their relationship by disobedience; she now invites him to repair their relationship by coming clean about what he did. So, too, God invites Adam to confession, to honest communication, and to restoration of the unity Adam had damaged.

How does Adam respond to the divine invitation? How does he respond to his call to confession? "[Adam] said, 'I heard the sound of you in the garden, and I was afraid, because I was naked; and I hid myself.' [God] said, 'Who told you that you were naked? Have you eaten from the tree of which I commanded you not to eat?' The man said, 'The woman whom you gave to be with me, she gave me fruit from the tree, and I ate'" (Gen. 3:10–13).

---

19. Peterson, "Biblical Series IV."
20. John Chrysostom, *Homilies on Genesis* 17.13, quoted *in Ancient Christian Commentaries on Scripture: Genesis 1–11*, 82–83.

When Adam fails to respond to the first invitation by God to a humble, honest admission of wrongdoing, God invites him very directly a second time: "Have you eaten from the tree of which I commanded you not to eat?" But Adam fails again. As Dorotheus of Gaza noted, "There was no change of heart but rather the contrary. He replied, 'The wife you gave me'—mark you, not 'my wife'—'deceived me.' 'The wife that *you* gave me,' as if to say, 'this disaster *you* placed on my head.'"[21]

The story of Adam is the story of everyone who does wrong and rationalizes the wrongdoing. "It's not my fault. My parents didn't raise me right. My boss is a pain. The wrong political party is in charge. Society is horrible . . ." To pass the blame rather than accept responsibility is the oldest human response to wrongdoing. Peterson notes that still today, it is not unusual for men to blame their problems on women:

> Adam's all innocent—except now, not only is he naked, disobedient, cowardly, and ashamed, he's also a sniveling, backbiting fink. He rats her out the second he gets the opportunity, and then he blames God. That's exactly right. You go online, and you read the commentary that men write about women when they're resentful and bitter about women. . . . "It's not me: it's them"—and not only that, but "What a bloody world this is in which they exist." It's exactly the same thing. It's exactly the same thing, and it is absolutely pathetic.[22]

If we deny that there is a problem, if we deny our role in the problem, how can we effectively deal with the problem? To deny personal responsibility is to compound our problems. To deny personal responsibility is, in many cases, to reject the only way out of the bad situation.

"Then the LORD God said to the woman, 'What is this that you have done?' The woman said, 'The serpent tricked me, and I ate'" (Gen. 3:13). Like

---

21. Dorotheus of Gaza, *Spiritual Instruction* 1, quoted in *Ancient Christian Commentaries on Scripture: Genesis 1–11*, 87.
22. Peterson, "Biblical Series IV."

Adam, Eve does not accept responsibility for her action. She too passes the blame onto someone else: the serpent. Who created the serpent? God. So Eve also implicitly blames God for her action. Like Ambrose and Justin Martyr before him, Peterson views Eve as relatively less guilty than Adam:

> Well, at least she has a bloody excuse. First of all, it's a snake. We already found out that they're subtle. Second, it turns out that the damn snake is Satan himself, and he's rather treacherous. So the fact that she got tangled up in his mess is, well, problematic, but it's a hell of a lot better excuse than Adam has.[23]

Whatever their relative level of guilt, Adam and Eve find themselves alienated from God, aware of their naked vulnerability before each other, and anxious about punishment.

Given that neither Adam nor Eve restores the unity they broke by means of honest communication, they suffer the consequences of disunity with God. God is always and unfailingly loving. But we are not, and when we are not loving God, we cause ourselves to suffer. God is akin to the sun, which always admits light and heat. But the light and heat of the sun, consistent as it is, can be experienced by us in radically different ways depending upon our own condition. If we are seated beside the pool, sipping a soda, and jumping in for a swim whenever we feel a little too hot, the rays of the sun feel wonderful to us. By contrast, on the same summer afternoon, if our car runs out of gas in the desert, and we have to walk fifteen miles to the gas station down a dirt road, the light and heat of the sun feel oppressive to us. The sun has not changed, but our relationship to the sun has changed. So, too, God's love is everlasting, but when we are in the desert of alienation from God, we experience God as wrathful and punishing. If God is the ultimate source of happiness, then when we separate ourselves from God, when we hide from God, we undermine our own happiness.

---

23. Peterson, "Biblical Series IV."

Peterson explores the consequences of the actions of Adam and Eve from another perspective. He cites Lynne A. Isbell's *The Fruit, the Tree, and the Serpent: Why We See So Well*, in which she argues that both the snake and the fruit are associated in our evolutionary past with increased vision and increased self-consciousness.[24] The self-consciousness of the human person is linked to the bigger brains of the human species. Bigger brains and relatively small female hips lead to the birth of helpless human children. Babies require intensive care if they are to survive. A birth mother always has a physical connection to her child and almost always has an intense bond to her baby. So the child's vulnerability leads also to a maternal vulnerability that facilitates male dominance.

Adam's punishment of toil for bread is also linked to self-consciousness. He realizes that however much he has today, tomorrow will come. Given his self-consciousness, Adam can imagine himself projected into the future. Adam now has concern for tomorrow: even if he has enough bread for today, that may not be true tomorrow, so he must work. The fall prompts Adam and Eve to sacrifice, to delay gratification for a higher good. Peterson notes, "The successful among us delay gratification. The successful among us bargain with the future."[25] To sacrifice is to give up something good now for the sake of something better in the future.

---

24. Lynne A. Isbell, *The Fruit, the Tree, and the Serpent: Why We See So Well* (Cambridge, MA: Harvard University Press, 2009).
25. Peterson, "Biblical Series V: Cain and Abel: The Hostile Brothers."

CHAPTER 4

Chaos, Utopia, and the
Divine Call to Adventure

Cain and Abel: What Hostile Brothers Can Teach Us

Peterson continues his rich biblical interpretation by considering the story of Cain and Abel. The archetypal brothers both suffer, but their radically different responses to their suffering represent perennial human options. After becoming self-conscious and leaving the Garden of Eden, "the man knew his wife Eve, and she conceived and bore Cain, saying, 'I have produced a man with the help of the LORD'" (Gen. 4:1). Cain is not just the firstborn son, Peterson notes, but the firstborn human being.

"Next she bore his brother Abel" (Gen. 4:2). In his book *The Beginning of Wisdom*, Leon Kass points out that Genesis records no joyous remarks, no gratitude to God, and no maternal pride accompanying Abel's birth.[1] Like most parents, Eve favors her firstborn.[2] Adam does too. "Now Abel was a keeper of sheep, and Cain a tiller of the ground" (Gen. 4:2). Adam cultivates the land and invites Cain to join him in the established family business. In ancient cultures, Peterson notes, the firstborn son inherited the land tilled by

---

1. Leon Kass, *The Beginning of Wisdom: Reading Genesis* (Notre Dame, IN: University of Notre Dame Press, 2006), 126.
2. Elsa Vulliamy, "Most Parents Have a Favourite Child and It's Likely to Be Their First-Born, Study Finds," *The Independent*, April 11, 2016, https://www.independent.co.uk/life-style/health-and-families/study-finds-more-two-thirds-parents-have-favourite-child-and-it-s-probably-their-first-born-a6978911.html.

his father, while the other sons had to fend for themselves. This practice had a strong rationale behind it: dividing the land equally among many sons would lead to increasingly small parcels of cultivated land available for farming over the generations, thereby increasing the likelihood of starvation for everyone.

So, with no mentor to guide him, Abel must make his way as a shepherd. The sheep like to wander where they will, and this draws him into potential conflict with Cain. Peterson points out,

> The herdsmen like to have their herds, sheep, cattle, go wherever they were going to go. The agriculturalists—the farmers—have things fenced off.[3]

The land provides Abel with less social support, more risk of violent death from wild animals, and greater exposure to the elements. So not just their rival social status in the family but also their occupations set Cain against Abel, with Abel getting the lesser part. How could Abel not notice Eve's favoritism, Adam's mentorship of his brother, and Cain's social status as firstborn? Abel is cast outside the home, relegated to keeping company with sheep. If a lion attacks him, who will hear his cry?

Abel's suffering drives him to self-development rather than despair. Peterson suggests that Abel "is ignorant and humble, and because of this, he can learn."[4] If you know that you don't know, that can be the beginning of the quest to know. If you think you know it all, then you think you have nothing left to learn. I know what this feels like. On my last day of kindergarten, on my walk home with two other kindergarteners, I announced to them, "Well, we're men now." I figured, I can write sentences. I can add and subtract. What else is there to learn?

Peterson's interpretation remains relatively silent about exactly what Abel learns and why he flourishes. Malcolm Gladwell's *David and Goliath* provides a possible answer. Armed with a sling and rocks, a good shepherd is a "slinger" who defends his sheep from lions and bears (see 1 Sam. 17:36).

---

3. Jordan Peterson, "Biblical Series V: Cain and Abel: The Hostile Brothers."
4. Peterson, "Biblical Series V."

"Imagine standing in front of a Major League Baseball pitcher as he aims a baseball at your head," writes Gladwell. "That's what facing a slinger was like—only what was being thrown was not a ball of cork and leather, but a solid rock."[5] Abel learned to defend the sheep and defend himself. If you've killed lions and bears, your older brother is not so intimidating. Rather than playing the victim, Abel becomes a warrior.

In his safe space tilling the land near home, Cain does not develop self-reliance or skill in violent means of protection. Abel gets stronger and stronger; Cain grows complacent and weak. "Abel is, by all appearances, dancing his way through life," writes Peterson. "Worst of all, he's genuinely a good person. Everyone knows it. He deserves his good fortune. All the more reason to envy and hate him."[6] Cain's envy intensifies.

"In the course of time, Cain brought to the LORD an offering of the fruit of the ground, and Abel for his part brought of the firstlings of his flock, their fat portions" (Gen. 4:3–4). Some modern readers might dismiss the idea of sacrifice as a superstitious practice of primitive savages, but Peterson offers a radically different interpretation. Our own suffering is undeniable, so what can we do about it? "If you want to make things better in the future," writes Peterson, "then you make sacrifices in the present." Human beings project their existence into the future, and so can work now to make their futures better. "It's our knowledge of the possibility of tragedy and suffering in the future that motivates us to sacrifice in the present, so that we can reduce the unnecessary anxiety, uncertainty, and pain that awaits us." Far from exhibiting primitive superstition, "the sacrifices that people were making to God were the dramatic precursors to the psychological idea of sacrifice that we all hold as civilized people in the modern world."[7]

To sacrifice is human, and to sacrifice for the sake of the greater good is to act with human wisdom. Writes Peterson:

---

5. Malcolm Gladwell, *David and Goliath: Underdogs, Misfits, and the Art of Battling Giants* (New York: Little & Brown, 2013), 10.
6. Jordan B. Peterson, *12 Rules for Life: An Antidote to Chaos* (New York: Penguin, 2019), 130.
7. This and the previous two quotations are taken from Peterson, "Biblical Series V."

Modern people have by no means stopped making sacrifices to God, regardless of what they think. Our very belief that hard work and discipline will bring success is a precise but abstracted and refined restatement of the idea that God will shower his grace on the individual who makes the right offering.[8]

"And the LORD had regard for Abel and his offering, but for Cain and his offering he had no regard" (Gen. 4:4–5). Like Augustine in the *City of God*, Peterson notes that it is unspecified why God prefers Abel's sacrifice. This nondisclosure in the story universalizes the message. We often do not know the reason why our sacrifices fail. We can set our minds to achieve some end, strive mightily in employing all available means at great cost, and come out with nothing but ashes.

"So Cain was very angry, and his countenance fell" (Gen. 4:5). Peterson comments:

> He becomes jealous and bitter—and it's no wonder. If someone fails and is rejected because he refused to make any sacrifices at all—well, that's at least understandable. He may still feel resentful and vengeful, but he knows in his heart that he is personally to blame. That knowledge generally places a limit on his outrage. It's much worse, however, if he had actually forgone the pleasures of the moment; if he had strived and toiled, and things still didn't work out; if he was rejected despite his efforts. Then his work—his sacrifice—has been pointless. Under such conditions, the world darkens, and the soul rebels.[9]

How does God respond to Cain's distress? "The LORD said to Cain, 'Why are you angry, and why has your countenance fallen? If you do well, will you not be accepted?'" (Gen. 4:6). God suggests that if Cain acts properly, Cain

---

8. Jordan B. Peterson, "A Psycho-ontological Analysis of Genesis 2–6," *Archive for the Psychology of Religion* 29 (2007): 114.

9. Peterson, *12 Rules for Life*, 128.

will be successful. The world is not against him. Indeed, the Creator of the world is trying to help him. He can do something about his predicament. He is not a helpless victim. God reminds Cain of his freedom. He can make the choice to make himself and the world better. To put his life in order, Cain needs to take responsibility.

God tells Cain, "And if you do not do well, sin is lurking at the door; its desire is for you, but you must master it" (Gen. 4:7). Peterson's interpretation of this passage is reminiscent of St. John Paul II's in *Evangelium Vitae*: "God, although preferring Abel's gift, does not interrupt his dialogue with Cain. He admonishes him, reminding him of his freedom in the face of evil: man is in no way predestined to evil. Certainly, like Adam, he is tempted by the malevolent force of sin which, like a wild beast, lies in wait at the door of his heart, ready to leap on its prey. But Cain remains free in the face of sin."[10]

Even now, Cain can shut the door on the predator. He can learn to be a slinger. He can take control of his life, make the proper sacrifices, and restore order. Cain doesn't like God's answer. Peterson notes,

> The last thing you want to hear if your life has turned into a catastrophe and you take God to task for creating a universe where that sort of thing was allowed, is that it's your own damn fault, and that you should straighten up and fly right, so to speak, and that you shouldn't be complaining about the nature of being. But that is the answer he gets.[11]

Cain's anger turns into rage against the injustice of the universe, rage against God. Cain would destroy the universe if he could. He would destroy God if he could. He will destroy Abel because he can. "Cain said to Abel his brother, 'Let us go out to the field'" (Gen. 4:8). Cain gets Abel alone, isolated from everyone else in the family. Cain knew that Abel, skilled in the use of

---

10. Pope John Paul II, *Evangelium Vitae*, 8, encyclical letter, Vatican website, March 25, 1995, http://www.vatican.va/content/john-paul-ii/en/encyclicals/documents/hf_jp-ii_enc_25031995_evangelium-vitae.html.

11. Peterson, "Biblical Series V."

violence against predators, could kill him. Cain is willing to risk his own destruction to commit premeditated murder.

"And when they were in the field, Cain rose up against his brother Abel and killed him" (Gen. 4:8). Rather than imitate his brother, Cain eliminates his brother. In Peterson's words, Cain commits "fratricidal murder—murder not only of someone innocent but of someone ideal and good, and murder done consciously to spite the creator of the universe."[12] Peterson points out that such malevolence against the innocent, the young, and the good is reenacted in various school shootings.

God sees the injustice of the world. "Then the LORD said to Cain, 'Where is your brother Abel?'" (Gen. 4:9). The question, of course, as with Adam and Eve in the garden, is not about Abel's physical location, but is an invitation to self-awareness and confession of wrongdoing. Cain replies to God, "I do not know; am I my brother's keeper?" (Gen. 4:9). Rather than a humble confession of guilt, Cain lies and implies that God is out of line in asking the question. Rounding out the sins noted by Peterson, St. Basil of Caesarea summarizes the ways Cain missed the mark: "The first sin is envy at the preference of Abel; the second is guile, whereby he said to his brother, Let us go into the field: the third is murder, a further wickedness: the fourth, fratricide, a still greater iniquity: the fifth that he committed the first murder, and set a bad example to mankind: the sixth wrong in that he grieved his parents: the seventh, his lie to God."[13] The capital vice of envy gives rise to these offspring. Sin begets sin.

"And the LORD said, 'What have you done? Listen; your brother's blood is crying out to me from the ground! And now you are cursed from the ground, which has opened its mouth to receive your brother's blood from your hand. When you till the ground, it will no longer yield to you its strength; you will be a fugitive and a wanderer on the earth'" (Gen. 4:10–12). After destroying his brother, an ideal man, Cain wanders the earth as a homeless fugitive,

---

12. Peterson, *12 Rules for Life*, 113.
13. Basil, *Letters* 260.3.

alienated from his parents, his work, and his homeland. Cain follows the pattern set by Adam and Eve. He refuses to answer honestly and denies personal responsibility by deflecting questions.

Filled with self-pity, the murderer casts himself as the victim cursed by an unforgivable sin. Thomas Aquinas, for one, disagrees with Cain's assessment of his situation: "Wherefore the words of Cain were reprehensible, when he said (Gen. 4:13): 'My iniquity is greater than that I may deserve pardon.' And so God's mercy, through Penance, grants pardon to sinners without any end."[14] Perhaps the greatest temptation for Cain and for people today is to consider their sins as beyond the power of God to forgive. Despair is a debilitating sin, for the person in despair refuses the remedy of seeking God's forgiveness. But the truth is, as Timothy Keller notes, "if you were a hundred times worse than you are, your sins would be no match for His mercy."[15] And the problem of Cain is a problem still for today. "People are every bit as dominated by shame and guilt today as they were in more traditional times, but they don't have the words for it anymore."[16] Without the words to label their disease, it is harder for people to find the cure of total forgiveness offered by God. Like Raskolnikov in Dostoyevsky's *Crime and Punishment*, Cain exemplifies the hellish state of the sinner who despairs. Cain manifests the insight of Augustine: "The punishment for sin is sin."[17]

But Cain is, in one way, in a better situation than Adam and Eve. They did not acknowledge the wrong they had done; Cain acknowledges his iniquity and the punishment that his sin deserves. We cannot deal with a problem unless we face it. Cain shows a bit of moral development in his awareness of his wrongdoing. Reconciliation begins with acknowledgment of wrongdoing.

---

14. Thomas Aquinas, *Summa theologiae* 3.84.10.

15. Timothy Keller, *The Prodigal Prophet: Jonah and the Mystery of God's Mercy* (New York: Viking, 2018), 211.

16. Timothy Keller, "People are every bit as dominated by shame and guilt today as they were in more traditional times, but they don't have the words for it anymore," Twitter, October 5, 2020, https://twitter.com/timkellernyc/status/1313179397617332224.

17. Augustine, *Against Julian*, ed. H. Dressler, trans. M.A. Schumacher (Washington, DC: The Catholic University of America Press, 1957), 254.

God responds with a severe mercy: "The Lord put a mark on Cain, so that no one who came upon him would kill him. Then Cain went away from the presence of the Lord, and settled in the land of Nod, east of Eden" (Gen. 4:15–16). God intervenes to circumvent what could have been the beginning of a cycle of violence. Brother kills brother. Friends of Abel kill Cain. Friends of Cain kill friends of Abel. And so on.

Cain and Abel represent rival responses to the fallen human condition. Self-consciousness gives rise to social comparison. Social comparison gives rise to suffering. Suffering can drive self-improvement or give rise to envy and its sins. Peterson writes,

> One brother, Abel, provides an early model for the redemptive Savior, as a genuine and voluntary incarnation of Logos. The other, Cain, refuses his responsibility, justifies that refusal with his existential pain and fear, and turns savage, destructive, corrupt, and murderous. Thus, two pathways of morality are laid out as primary modes of ethical being, in a world composed of the interplay between chaos and order.[18]

In Peterson's view,

> The story of Cain and Abel is one manifestation of the archetypal tale of hostile brothers, hero and adversary: the two elements of the individual human psyche, one aimed up, at the good, and the other, down, at hell itself.[19]

Peterson echoes Augustine, who saw Abel as a citizen of the heavenly City of God and Cain as a citizen of the hellish City of Man.

Some people tend to see themselves as Abel—as innocent victims. All their problems are someone else's fault. But Peterson holds that anyone can be Cain. It is harder to recognize the ways in which we have harmed others

---

18. Peterson, "Psycho-ontological Analysis," 123.
19. Peterson, *12 Rules for Life*, 129.

by what we've done or what we've failed to do. The lessons of Germany's Reserve Police Battalion 101, Solzhenitsyn's *Gulag Archipelago*, and Milgram's obedience experiment suggest that Peterson is right. The potential for great evil, and often the reality of great evil, is within us all.

The Flood of Noah and the Inevitable Chaos of Our Lives

Having previously looked at his understanding of Adam and Eve as well as Cain and Abel, this section explicates and develops Peterson's interpretation of the story of Noah and the flood. While acknowledging reports of an ancient flood present in many different cultures, Peterson focuses on what the story of Noah means for us today. In offering an interpretation that goes beyond the historical, Peterson follows in the footsteps of Jerome, Origen, and Cyprian. Augustine once said, "Nowhere in the Gospel do we read that the Lord said: 'I am sending you a Paraclete who will teach you about the course of the sun and the moon.' For He wanted to make Christians, not mathematicians."[20] The purpose of the story of Noah is not to make us historians of ancient rainfall patterns. So, what can we learn from Noah and the flood?

The story begins with a claim as fresh as this morning's news: "The wickedness of humankind was great in the earth" (Gen. 6:5). In considering the gulags and the concentration camps, it is hard to deny human wickedness. Nor do we not have to look to Soviet Communists or Nazi brownshirts to find deep depravity. Sooner or later, notes Peterson, "you'll tangle with someone who's malevolent right to the core, and maybe it'll be you that is malevolent."[21] The man in the mirror can prove Peterson's point.

The story continues: "And the LORD was sorry that he had made humankind on the earth, and it grieved him to his heart. So the LORD said, 'I will blot out from the earth the human beings I have created—people together with animals and creeping things and birds of the air, for I am sorry that I

20. Augustine, "A Debate with Felix the Manichean" 1.10, quoted in *The Faith of the Early Fathers*, trans. W.A. Jurgens, vol. 3 (Collegeville, MN: Liturgical Press, 1979), 88.
21. Peterson, "Biblical Series VII: Walking with God: Noah and the Flood."

have made them'" (Gen. 6:7). God goes from delighting in creation earlier in Genesis to sorrowing over creation. Does God really change? Peterson does not take up this question, but let us consider it.

Classic Christian theology holds that God's love is unchangingly faithful. The love of God is like the work of a good doctor. A good doctor unfailingly aims to help us become healthy. But if we are overweight, smoking five packs a day, and eating only Twinkies, a good doctor will challenge us to change to a healthier lifestyle. A good doctor may even appear to us as threatening in warning us that we will suffer illness and even death unless we change. In a similar way, God's love is unchangingly faithful. Our relationship with the God who is Truth feels heavenly or hellish depending on our spiritual condition. As Augustine noted, "They love truth when it enlightens them, they hate truth when it accuses them."[22] From the perspective of those doing injustice, they perceive God as an angry enemy who sorrows over creating mankind.

Not everyone, however, viewed God as an enemy. "Noah was a righteous man, blameless in his generation; Noah walked with God" (Gen. 6:9). What does it mean to walk with God? Peterson describes Christ's Sermon on the Mount as "the closest thing we have to a fully articulated description of what it would mean to walk with God, so that you're in the ark when the flood comes."[23] To be merciful, to be pure of heart, to be a peacemaker is to walk with God. To imitate Christ daily, according to Peterson, is to build an ark so as to save ourselves, our family, and the goodness of creation.

But whether we are like Noah building an ark or we are like his corrupt contemporaries, Peterson highlights an undeniable reality: "There are floods coming. You can bloody well be sure of that."[24] The downpour of diseases, disasters, and deaths will surely afflict us all. Our suffering is a certainty. To obey conscience is to prepare for the flood. Peterson suggests, "This is a form of prayer. Sit on your bed one day and ask yourself, 'What remarkably stupid

---

22. Augustine, *Confessions* (Park Ridge, IL: Word on Fire Classics, 2017), 256.
23. Peterson, "Biblical Series VII."
24. Peterson, "Biblical Series VI: The Psychology of the Flood."

things am I doing on a regular basis to absolutely screw up my life?'"[25] When we honestly ask what we can do better, we quickly find out that we are not living according to our highest and best ideals. To build an ark is to live in accordance with those highest and best ideals. "Every day is judgment day," on Peterson's view. "The part of you that's equivalent to the logos, the part of you that's your own ideal, sits in eternal judgment on your iniquity."[26] In this, Peterson echoes the thought of John Henry Newman, who said, "Conscience is the aboriginal Vicar of Christ."[27]

The story continues, "The Lord said to Noah, 'For in seven days I will send rain on the earth for forty days and forty nights'" (Gen. 7:4). The chaos emerging from disharmony with the Creator is poetically represented by the primordial waters falling from the sky. The story of the flood, in other words, is not a tale of God becoming frustrated and lashing out at human beings. The flood represents the consequences of disharmony with God. In acting out of harmony with divine love, we cause primordial chaos within ourselves. When we act against our ideals, we create within ourselves an inner schizophrenia. We pit the best of ourselves against the rest of ourselves.

This inner chaos spills out. As Eleonore Stump points out in her magisterial book *Wandering in Darkness*, self-alienation undermines our relationships with other people and with God.[28] When we are self-divided, we are double-minded and mixed in motive. We cannot wholeheartedly love others, since our heart is itself divided. Our inner division afflicts the ones we love, causing floods in their lives and ours. And even when our actions do not directly cause the flood, our actions (including our failure to prepare) can make the inevitable floods of life much worse.

According to Genesis, the rains and the flood do not last forever. Fellow psychologist Martin Seligman's work on what he called "learned helplessness"

---

25. Peterson, "Biblical Series VII."

26. Peterson, "Biblical Series VII."

27. John Henry Newman, *Certain Difficulties Felt by Anglicans in Catholic Teaching Considered*, vol. 2 (New York: Longmans & Green, 1900), 248, http://www.newmanreader.org/works/anglicans/volume2/gladstone/.

28. Eleonore Stump, *Wandering in Darkness: Narrative and the Problem of Suffering* (New York: Oxford University Press, 2010).

develops Peterson's interpretation.[29] When encountering the floods of life, some people believe that their troubles will last forever, that the rains will ruin everything, and that there is nothing that they can do about it. A person with Christian hope has a remedy for learned helplessness. No rain lasts forever, since no earthly suffering continues after death. Nor can any flood undermine the hope of eternal life. And finally, there is always something that we can do about the chaotic waters of life. God helps his people to build an ark, to make the best of the worst.

After forty days, the rain stops, and the flood recedes. God says to Noah, "Go out of the ark, you and your wife, and your sons and your sons' wives with you" (Gen. 8:16). By obeying conscience, by building an ark, Noah saves himself, his family, and the created order. Peterson says,

> If you walk properly, aim properly, act properly, and act with God in the manner that we've been discussing, perhaps that isn't only for you. Perhaps it's also the thing that will save your family. And then, by implication, perhaps it will also save society.[30]

The good that we do has ramifications beyond our calculations.

The Tower of Babel and the Utopia of Reason

Peterson sees the story of the Tower of Babel as a warning about the dangers of idolizing the intellect in utopian attempts to make heaven on earth. Coming after Noah and the flood, the story of the Tower of Babel begins, "Now the whole earth had one language and the same words" (Gen. 11:1). These first people said, "Come, let us build ourselves a city, and a tower with its top in the heavens, and let us make a name for ourselves, lest we be scattered abroad upon the face of the whole earth" (Gen. 11:4). In Peterson's view, they

---

29. See, for example, *Authentic Happiness* (New York: Free Press, 2002) and *Learned Optimism* (New York: Vintage Books, 2006).
30. Peterson, "Biblical Series VII."

want to create a path to heaven, and ultimately to "build a structure that's so large and encompassing that it can replace heaven itself."[31] Using their reason, they seek a utopia.

God intervenes: "And the LORD came down to see the city and the tower, which mortals had built" (Gen. 11:5). According to Augustine in the *City of God*, this language should not be understood simplistically. God does not "come down," understood as moving in spatial location. God is not a material body limited and confined to one location. Likewise, God cannot be ignorant of anything. As Thomas Aquinas notes, God knows everything in creation, not by looking outward and seeing things, but by knowing himself perfectly from all eternity as First Cause, Prime Mover, and Creator.

> And the LORD said, "Look, they are one people, and they have all one language; and this is only the beginning of what they will do; nothing that they propose to do will now be impossible for them. Come, let us go down, and confuse their language there, so that they will not understand one another's speech." So the LORD scattered them abroad from there over the face of all the earth, and they left off building the city. Therefore it was called Babel, because there the LORD confused the language of all the earth; and from there the LORD scattered them abroad over the face of all the earth. (Gen. 11:6–9)

Peterson notes that this passage seems to portray God as jealous and petty. But if God is all-good, all-wise, and all-loving, God cannot do evil, unwise, and petty actions. So, what is going on here?

Peterson sees the story as a warning about idolizing the intellect (rationalism) and pursuing heaven on earth (utopia). Rationalism makes reason an idol to replace God. It should be noted, however, that a warning about rationalism is *not* condemning reason. Unlike some religious traditions, the Catholic Church champions the compatibility of faith and reason, including the study of philosophy (the love of wisdom). St. John Paul II dedicated an

---

31. Peterson, "Biblical Series VIII: Phenomenology of the Divine."

entire encyclical to the proposition that "faith and reason are like two wings on which the human spirit rises to the contemplation of truth; and God has placed in the human heart a desire to know the truth—in a word, to know himself—so that, by knowing and loving God, men and women may also come to the fullness of truth about themselves."[32] The Church founded universities in the eleventh century. Likewise, it is a myth that that the Church opposes science.[33] But *rationalism* goes much further than upholding the value of reason; it considers reason *alone* as all that is needed for human flourishing. Rationalism rejects grace, rejects revelation, and downplays the reality of human weakness. As Jordan Peterson notes, "The arrogance of the intellect—that's the thing the Catholic Church has warned about for centuries."[34]

In *Paradise Lost*, Milton's Satan represents this rationalistic approach. As the greatest of all created minds, the devil thinks that he has no need of God. Peterson notes that Milton

> had intimations of what was coming, as human rationality and technology became more and more powerful. The intimation was that we would produce systems that dispensed with God, that were completely rational, that were completely total, and that would immediately turn everything they touched into something indistinguishable from hell. Milton's warning, embodied in the poem, is that the rational mind that generates a production, and then worships it as if it's absolute, immediately occupies hell.[35]

Those who worship the intellect think reason alone provides all that the human person needs for full flourishing.

---

32. Pope John Paul II, *Fides et Ratio*, preface, encyclical letter, Vatican website, September 14, 1998, http://www.vatican.va/content/john-paul-ii/en/encyclicals/documents/hf_jp-ii_enc_14091998_fides-et-ratio.html.

33. See Christopher Kaczor, *The Seven Big Myths about the Catholic Church* (San Francisco: Ignatius Press, 2012), 19–36.

34. Bite-sized Philosophy, "Jordan Peterson—The Arrogance of the Intellect," YouTube video, 2:18, https://youtu.be/txyINNJU6Qc.

35. Peterson, "Biblical Series VIII."

In fact, knowledge alone cannot establish the best condition possible—namely, salvation. Knowledge alone does not make us good. To *know* what is right is one thing. To *do* what is right is something else, requiring not just knowledge but virtue. Knowledge alone cannot perfect our relationship with God or with human beings.

The Tower of Babel is also a symbol of utopia. God interrupts the building in Babel because utopian dreams of heaven on earth actually bring about hell on earth. In efforts to bring about utopia, totalitarians seek strict uniformity in speech and action. Individuals who do not conform are punished or even killed. As Walter Duranty, the *New York Times* reporter turned apologist for Joseph Stalin, put it, "You can't make an omelet without breaking eggs"[36]—or, in the case of Communist attempts to create utopia, without killing more than eighty-five million people (and counting).

Peterson provides powerful critiques of utopian visions. First, utopian visions of equality of outcome seek the impossible. In every area, among human beings and lobsters alike, dominance hierarchies spontaneously emerge. Individuals must seek something valuable to remain alive. Whether it is hunting wild buffalo, harvesting maize corn, or harnessing solar energy, some individuals are better at pursuing what they seek than others. As economist Thomas Sowell points out in *Discrimination and Disparities*, inequality of outcome results from numerous factors out of our control: "If there is not equality among people born to the same parents and raised under the same roof, why should equality of outcomes be expected—or assumed—when conditions are not nearly so comparable?"[37] Having been tried for more than a hundred years in countries all over the world, the utopian goal of equality of outcomes brings about tyranny rather than equality of outcomes.

Second, utopian dreamers lack humility about their knowledge. Large social systems are extremely complex, and any intervention may bring about unintended and unwanted consequences. Rather than concentrating power

---

36. Quoted in "New York Times Statement About 1932 Pulitzer Prize Awarded to Walter Duranty," The New York Times Company website, https://www.nytco.com/company/prizes-awards/new-york-times-statement-about-1932-pulitzer-prize-awarded-to-walter-duranty/.

37. Thomas Sowell, *Discrimination and Disparities* (New York: Basic Books, 2019), 7.

in central command, it is much better to leave decision-making in the hands of those closest to the realities in question. They know the local situation best. In Catholic thought, the utopian temptation to an all-embracing world order is contradicted by the principle of subsidiarity: "Neither the state nor any larger society should substitute itself for the initiative and responsibility of individuals and intermediary bodies."[38]

Third, some individuals focus on the problems outside of themselves because it is (initially) easier than dealing with the man in the mirror. As Peterson notes,

> All of you who made announcements to yourself every January about changing your diet and going to the gym know perfectly well how difficult it is to regulate your own impulses and to bring yourself under the control of some ethical and attentive structure of values. It's extraordinarily difficult. People don't do it. Instead, they wander off, and I think they create towers of Babel.[39]

If we cannot even perfect ourselves as individuals, how can we possibly perfect society as a whole? Isn't society made up of individuals? If they are not perfect, how can what they make up be perfect?

Fourth, focusing on a utopian vision distracts us from significant improvements that are actually possible to achieve. Unlike establishing a utopia, we can actually become a better version of ourselves. For this reason, *12 Rules for Life* focuses on taking personal responsibility for what we do in daily life.

Finally, in *Notes from the Underground*, Dostoevsky imagines what would take place if we ever did create utopia. He thinks we would be dissatisfied and smash the utopia in order to enjoy the unexpected adventure of life.[40]

In every generation, we are tempted to idolize the intellect. In every

---

38. *Catechism of the Catholic Church*, 1883.
39. Peterson, "Biblical Series VIII."
40. Fyodor Dostoevsky, *Notes from the Underground*, trans. Constance Garnett (Indianapolis, IN: Hackett, 2009).

generation, we are tempted to create a utopian heaven on earth. The Tower of Babel is therefore a story of everlasting relevance.

The Call to Heroic Adventure: Abraham and Ourselves

According to Peterson, the story of the call of Abraham is not just about an ancient nomad. It embodies archetypal insights about the call to every individual to become a hero. Abraham's vocation does not preserve him from deep suffering, nor from serious sinning, but it does lead to ultimate salvation for him and his family.

"Now the LORD said to Abram, 'Go from your country and your kindred and your father's house to the land that I will show you. I will make of you a great nation, and I will bless you, and make your name great, so that you will be a blessing'" (Gen. 12:1–2). God calls the comfortable Abram to become the heroic Abraham. The change of name indicates a change of heart, a willingness to take on responsibility for an ideal. God calls him to leave the safe space of his childhood home for an adventure in an unknown territory. God calls him to be a hero. As Rabbi Jonathan Sacks notes,

> Abraham is without doubt the most influential person who ever lived. Today he is claimed as the spiritual ancestor of 2.3 billion Christians, 1.8 billion Muslims and 14 million Jews, more than half the people alive today. Yet he ruled no empire, commanded no great army, performed no miracles and proclaimed no prophecy. He is the supreme example in all of history of *influence without power.* Why? Because he was prepared to be different. . . .
>
> The majority is not always right and conventional wisdom is not always wise. Dead fish go with the flow. Live fish swim against the current. So it is with conscience and courage. So it is with the children of Abraham. They are prepared to challenge the idols of the age.[41]

---

41. Jonathan Sacks, "The Courage Not to Conform," Jonathan Sacks (website), October 26, 2020, https://rabbisacks.org/lech-lecha-5781/.

God's call to be a hero is a vocation given to everyone. As St. John Paul II noted, God "stirs in you the desire to do something great with your lives, the will to follow an ideal, the refusal to allow yourselves to be ground down by mediocrity, the courage to commit yourselves humbly and patiently to improving yourselves and society, making the world more human and more fraternal."[42] The specifics of the heroic call vary greatly. Abraham was called to leave his homeland and to become the father of a great nation. Mary was called to be the mother of Jesus and to be the mother of all God's adopted children. Mother Teresa was called to minister to the poorest of the poor and to inspire millions with her example. As Germain Grisez notes in his book *Personal Vocation*, God calls everyone to follow the universal call of love, but this call is carried out in a totally unique, specific way for each individual. "God has created me to do Him some definite service," said John Henry Cardinal Newman. "He has committed some work to me which He has not committed to another. I have my mission."[43] Holocaust survivor and psychologist Victor Frankl echoed the insight: "Everyone has his own specific vocation or mission in life; everyone must carry out a concrete assignment that demands fulfillment. Therein he cannot be replaced, nor can his life be repeated. Thus, everyone's task is unique as is his specific opportunity to implement it."[44]

The adventure of the hero's life is to discover, embrace, and live out personal responsibility. If we live out personal responsibility, we will voluntarily embrace suffering. Jesus said, "Take up *your* cross and follow me" (see Matt. 16:24; emphasis added). Every cross is unique. Fr. Paul Mankowski notes, "I have never yet met anyone who thought that God gave him the right cross to bear (including myself); everyone looks around with a certain wistful envy at others and says to himself, 'Now THAT is the kind of cross I could

---

42. John Paul II, "15th World Youth Day Address of the Holy Father John Paul II at the Vigil of Prayer," Vatican website, August 19, 2000, http://www.vatican.va/content/john-paul-ii/en/speeches/2000/jul-sep/documents/hf_jp-ii_spe_20000819_gmg-veglia.html.

43. John Henry Newman, *Meditations and Devotions of the Late Cardinal Newman* (New York: Longmans & Green, 1907), 301, http://www.newmanreader.org/works/meditations/meditations9.html.

44. Viktor Frankl, *Man's Search for Meaning* (Boston: Beacon, 2000), 109.

carry with equanimity, courage, even joy.' But of course what makes a cross a cross is that it kills the one who carries it; it puts to death that part of the disciple that God knows must die for salvation to work."[45] Abraham's cross is Abraham's, Peterson's cross is Peterson's, and your cross is yours.

Along with his wife Sarah and his nephew Lot, Abraham leaves the comforts of home. He enters a land stricken by famine, surrounded by powerful men who want to sleep with his wife, and ruled by a tyrannous Pharaoh. Lot and Abraham fight with each other and part ways. Sarah and Abraham struggle with infertility. Abraham's faith in God is tested. How can God make him the father of a great nation, if he does not even have a single child? Abraham faces challenges that stretch him beyond what he can see.

So, too, with anyone who embraces his or her personal vocation. Every hero encounters formidable challenges. As Peterson notes,

> [Abraham] enters into a covenant with God to act in the world. The action is an adventure story, essentially. The adventures repeat, and they're punctuated by success and sacrifice and re-contemplation. It's the hero's journey uphill: I'm here; there's a crisis; I collapse; I reconstruct myself to a higher place. Life is like that, continually, and that's the story of Abraham.[46]

The story of every man and every woman is something like the adventure of a hero: facing challenges, being confronted by the dragon of chaos, and engaging in the fight of a lifetime.

What makes a person a hero is a deliberate response to the inevitable sufferings and setbacks encountered when pursuing an ideal. As John Henry Newman writes, "If I am in sickness, my sickness may serve Him, in perplexity, my perplexity may serve Him. If I am in sorrow, my sorrow may serve Him. He does nothing in vain. He knows what He is about. He may take away my friends. He may throw me among strangers. He may make

---

45. Quoted in Rod Dreher, "The Life and Death of Paul Mankowski," The American Conservative, September 10, 2020, https://www.theamericanconservative.com/dreher/life-and-death-of-paul-mankowski-sj/.

46. Peterson, "Biblical Series IX: The Call to Abraham."

me feel desolate, make my spirits sink, hide my future from me. Still, He knows what He is about."[47] The inevitable crises, setbacks, and downturns do not destroy the providence of God to bring good out of evil, to make heroes of us all.

Abraham's difficulties come not just from exterior forces like powerful men and deadly famine but also from his personal missteps and sins. At one point, to protect himself, Abraham lies by saying that his beautiful wife is his sister. He lets her be taken into the Pharaoh's house of harem women. Later, at his wife's prompting, Abraham fathers a child, Ishmael, with another woman, Hagar. These actions lead to calamitous consequences for Hagar, Ishmael, Sarah, and Abraham.

But even these serious flaws do not ultimately undermine Abraham's heroic mission. As Peterson notes,

> That's good news for everyone, because perfect people are very, very hard to find. If the only pathway to having a rich and meaningful life was through perfection, then we would all be in deep trouble.[48]

To be a hero is not to be perfect. No one now walking on earth has achieved the perfection of heaven. And yet, notes Peterson, "if you're aligned with God, and you pay attention to the divine injunction, then you can operate in the midst of chaos, tyranny, and deception, and flourish. You could hardly hope to have a better piece of news than that, given that that's exactly where you are."[49] As Pope Benedict XVI noted, "If you follow the will of God, you know that in spite of all the terrible things that happen to you, you will never lose a final refuge. You know that the foundation of the world is love, so that even when no human being can or will help you, you may go on, trusting in the One who loves you."[50]

---

47. Newman, *Meditations and Devotions*, 301–302.
48. Peterson, "Biblical Series IX."
49. Peterson, "Biblical Series IX."
50. Joseph Ratzinger, *Jesus of Nazareth: From the Baptism in the Jordan to the Transfiguration* (New York: Doubleday, 2007), 38.

The implications of the divine call, each individual's personal vocation, expand exponentially outward. What difference could I make for myself, for my family, for those I love, if I brought the best of myself to the world? What would happen if I really listened to the divine call? Peterson notes,

> My sense, instead, is that if you are able to reveal the best of yourself to you and the world, that you would be an overwhelming force for good. Whatever errors that might be made along the way would wash out in the works.[51]

The heroic individual, despite exterior foes and inner faults, journeys toward the promised land, accompanied by those he loves. Abraham, our father in faith, models the response of a hero engaged in the adventure of life.

---

51. Peterson, "Biblical Series IX."

CHAPTER 5

Myth Become Fact

Having looked in detail at Peterson's analysis of Genesis, it should be clear that his rich and appealing approach to Scripture—one rooted in scientific, literary, and tropological interpretation—has many points of contact with the Christian tradition. Nevertheless, the question remains: Where does Peterson's scriptural analysis, from a Christian perspective, fall short? As noted in the introduction, a Christian approach to Scripture includes but goes beyond Peterson's approach—it includes not only the moral sense of Scripture but other senses as well. The *Catechism of the Catholic Church* presents these as follows:

> According to an ancient tradition, one can distinguish between two *senses* of Scripture: the literal and the spiritual, the latter being subdivided into the allegorical, moral and anagogical senses. The profound concordance of the four senses guarantees all its richness to the living reading of Scripture in the Church.
>
> The *literal sense* is the meaning conveyed by the words of Scripture and discovered by exegesis, following the rules of sound interpretation: "All other senses of Sacred Scripture are based on the literal."
>
> The *spiritual sense.* Thanks to the unity of God's plan, not only the text of Scripture but also the realities and events about which it speaks can be signs.
>
> 1. The *allegorical sense.* We can acquire a more profound understanding of events by recognizing their significance in Christ; thus the

crossing of the Red Sea is a sign or type of Christ's victory and also of Christian Baptism.

2. The *moral sense.* The events reported in Scripture ought to lead us to act justly. As St. Paul says, they were written "for our instruction."

3. The *anagogical sense* (Greek: *anagoge*, "leading"). We can view realities and events in terms of their eternal significance, leading us toward our true homeland: thus the Church on earth is a sign of the heavenly Jerusalem.[1]

Thus, Peterson's approach to Scripture, while expanding on modern literalism, still is limited; it gives us only a piece of the even richer and even more complex Christian tradition. This tradition *includes* Peterson's approach, but goes beyond it. Exploring the various dimensions of these senses and their application throughout the history of scriptural interpretation would take us beyond the scope of this book. For a more succinct but still compelling answer to this question, we turn to one of the most persuasive Christian apologists of the twentieth century, a man who understood in his bones the crucial difference between Christianity and myth.

Jordan Peterson and C.S. Lewis on Myth and Truth

C.S. Lewis was a professor of literature who explained Christianity to secular audiences. Peterson is a professor of psychology who explains the Bible, especially the stories of Genesis, in ways that resonate with secular audiences. Both Peterson and Lewis appreciate the power of myth. But what is "myth" exactly? Myth is an ambiguous term. Myth is sometimes used to mean an entertaining but silly story naïve people made up to explain what they did not understand. We could call this "myth as *narrative theoretical ignorance.*" Myth, in this sense of the term, is of its very nature opposed to facts, science, and truth. On the other hand, myth is sometimes

---

1. *Catechism of the Catholic Church*, 115–117.

used to mean a poetic, narrative embodiment of deep insight for human living. We could call this "myth as *narrative practical wisdom*." Myth in this sense goes beyond the empirically verifiable but is not opposed to the facts found by science.

Myth as narrative practical wisdom embodies what is important to us, and what is important to us goes beyond what can be empirically verifiable—and it is this understanding of myth with which Peterson is concerned. As Peterson puts it,

> In the mythological world, what matters is what's important. The world is made out of what matters, not of matter. It requires a very different orientation.[2]

Albert Einstein is said to have made a similar point: "Not everything that can be counted counts, and not everything that counts can be counted."[3] So, insofar as we act, we all necessarily live in the mythological world—that is, a world not reducible simply to the scientific method and what is empirically verifiable. The world as investigated by science does not give us enough information to act in the world. You might liken science to an excellent doctor who can detect illness and health. An excellent doctor is invaluable. But medical expertise does not cover the entirety of human life. The doctor as doctor is not expert in investing money, hitting a baseball, making a marriage work, or learning Spanish. If all we have is medicine, if all we have is science, many important facets of life remain unilluminated.

Inasmuch as we must act in the world, we embody a view about what is valuable and what is not. Peterson says,

---

2. "335: Exploring Archetypes with Jordan B. Peterson," *The Art of Manliness* podcast, August 31, 2017 (updated February 3, 2021), https://www.artofmanliness.com/articles/podcast-335-using-power-myths-live-flourishing-life/.

3. "Attributed to Einstein: Probably Not by Einstein," *The Ultimate Quotable Einstein*, ed. Alice Calaprice (Princeton, NJ: Princeton University Press, 2010), 482.

Everybody acts out a myth, but very few people know what their myth is. You should know what your myth is, because it might be a tragedy, and maybe you don't want it to be. That's really worth thinking about, because you have a pattern of behavior that characterizes you.[4]

Every culture has its myths because every culture embodies characteristic patterns of action. Inasmuch as there is a shared human nature, we would expect these stories to share commonalities. Peterson explains,

Because we're all human and because we all share the same biological platform, a platform that we share even with animals to a large degree, we tend to interpret the world in very similar ways. Those interpretations are often expressed in stories. The stories are descriptions about how human beings act, and our fundamental problem in the world is how to act.[5]

We can find similarities, therefore, between Christian stories and pagan stories, between narrative practical wisdom as articulated by the children of Abraham and narrative practical wisdom as articulated by the children of Homer. Nor are these myths confined to the ancient world. Notes Peterson,

They manifest themselves everywhere. They manifest themselves in movies and in books. I mean, *Harry Potter* is a mythological story. It made Rowling richer than the Queen of England. You know, these stories have power.[6]

We find mythical narratives in *Sleeping Beauty*, *The Lion King*, and *Beauty and the Beast*.

Lewis and Peterson agree that the Christian narrative is something special, but for different reasons. According to Peterson,

---

4. Peterson, "Biblical Series I: Introduction to the Idea of God."

5. "335: Exploring Archetypes with Jordan B. Peterson," *The Art of Manliness* podcast.

6. "Joe Rogan Experience 1070–Jordan Peterson Transcript," *Erika Mentari* (blog), February 27, 2018, https://erikamentari.wordpress.com/2018/02/27/jre-1070-jordan-peterson-transcript/.

Christianity has done two things: it's developed the most explicit doctrine of good versus evil, and it's developed the most explicit and articulated doctrine of the logos. And so I would say, in many traditions, it's implicit. It's implicit in hero mythology, for example. I think what happens is that, if you aggregate enough hero myths and extract out the central theme, you end up with the logos. It's the thing that's common to all heroes.[7]

If you look at the story of the hero as told by pagan myths and in Hebrew writings, and extract the greatest characteristics of all these heroes, the greatest of all heroes is Christ. Lewis would certainly agree, but Lewis provides another explanation of the greatness of Christ.

Peterson declines to affirm or deny life after death:

I'm not making any claims at the moment about metaphysics or post-life existence. I'm saying that these descriptions pertain to psychological conditions that are always around us, right here and now, and that the mythological landscape is the landscape of human experience. It's not the objective world. The landscape of human experience and the objective world aren't the same thing.[8]

Lewis, as an explicitly believing Christian, of course affirms life after death, which makes Christ the hero an even greater figure. Christ takes on the greatest responsibility and overcomes the greatest threat. The greatest threat is not pain of a limited time and duration. The greatest threat is not even death. The greatest threat is unlimited pain for an unlimited duration in an unending death. Christians call this hell. Christ offers salvation from hell. Moreover, Christ the hero saves not just his family, as did Noah, and not just his nation, as did David; Christ offers salvation to every human being.

---

7. Jordan Peterson, "Ideology, Logos and Belief: A Discussion with Transliminal Media," Jordan B. Peterson (website), https://www.jordanbpeterson.com/transcripts/transliminal/.
8. "335: Exploring Archetypes with Jordan B. Peterson," *The Art of Manliness* podcast.

Most importantly, Peterson and Lewis diverge on whether the narrative practical wisdom of the Christian narrative is also objectively, historically, and literally true. On Lewis' view,

> The heart of Christianity is a myth which is also a fact. The old myth of the Dying God, *without ceasing to be myth*, comes down from the heaven of legend and imagination to the earth of history. It happens—at a particular date, in a particular place, followed by definable historical consequences. We pass from a Balder or an Osiris, dying nobody knows when or where, to a historical Person crucified (it is all in order) under Pontius Pilate. By becoming fact it does not cease to be myth: that is the miracle.[9]

Peterson seems, at least so far, to be still considering the question of whether the myth is also a fact. When asked if he has faith, Peterson sometimes replies that he strives to live as if God exists. C.S. Lewis himself had a striking analysis of such a striving in *Mere Christianity*—which, though about the love of God, is intertwined with belief:

> Some writers use the word charity to describe not only Christian love between human beings, but also God's love for man and man's love for God. About the second of these two, people are often worried. They are told they ought to love God. They cannot find any such feeling in themselves. What are they to do? The answer is the same as before. Act as if you did. Do not sit trying to manufacture feelings. Ask yourself, "If I were sure that I loved God what would I do?" When you have found the answer, go and do it.[10]

Or, as Fr. Richard John Neuhaus put it succinctly: "If you would believe," he said, "act as though you believe, leaving it to God to know whether you believe, for such leaving it to God is faith."[11]

---

9. C.S. Lewis, *God in the Dock: Essays on Theology and Ethics* (Grand Rapids, MI: Eerdmans, 1970), 66–67.

10. C.S. Lewis, *Mere Christianity* (New York: HarperOne, 2001), 132.

11. Quoted in Randy Boyagoda, "Cordially, Richard John Neuhaus," *First Things*, August 2012, https://www.firstthings.com/article/2012/08/cordially-richard-john-neuhaus.

If living as if God exists is already faith, then perhaps this faith can also lead to a faith that the myth became fact.

PART II

A Christian Response
to *12 Rules for Life*

Matthew R. Petrusek

CHAPTER 6

In the Parking Lot, Outside the Church: Jordan Peterson's Theology

Jordan Peterson—the man most responsible for reintroducing "God talk" into mainstream secular culture—balks when asked if he's a believer: "I live," Peterson repeats, usually after a pensive silence, "as if God exists."

As if he exists. By itself, the response sounds superficial, even juvenile. It can invite the criticism that the man who counsels everyone to stand up straight acts like a philosophical slouch when pressed on his own beliefs. Yet there's not only authenticity in Peterson's answer. There's wisdom—a wisdom, in fact, that finds voice in a surprising ally: Pope Emeritus Benedict XVI. Addressing a Europe increasingly dismissive of God, Benedict writes, "Even the one who does not succeed in finding the path to accepting the existence of God ought nevertheless to try to live and to direct his life *veluti si Deus daretur*, as if God did indeed exist."[1]

Again, *as if he exists.* This is not, as critics suggest, a crass soteriological cost-benefit analysis. Like everyone who takes the question of God seriously, Benedict understands that it's not just your life (and eternal life) that hangs in the balance. If unbelief reaches a critical mass, it ends up affecting everyone. The private may not be the public on all issues, but it certainly is on the question of God. It is for this reason that Benedict, having witnessed a virulent secularity hollow out his cherished Europe—the Europe that Christianity

---

1. Joseph Ratzinger, *Christianity and the Crisis of Cultures*, trans. Brian McNeil (San Francisco: Ignatius Press, 2006), 51.

built, and in fact, the Europe that made secularity possible by laying down the foundations for individual dignity and autonomous civil authority in the first place—devoted much of his papacy to stemming the bleed of unbelief into the civil sphere. The endgame has come into sharper focus as the downfall accelerates. Benedict sounds the alarm, because he rightly observes that it's only a matter of time before the theologically emancipated begin torching *all* institutions, including, but not limited to, the institutional church, in the name of "freedom." As he observes, "[Modern] man enters the world no longer as a gift of the Creator, but as the product of our activity—and a product that can be selected according to requirements that we ourselves stipulate."[2]

But what should we stipulate? And how do we come up with the "requirements"? That's precisely the problem. With the death of God, Friedrich Nietzsche, with a hat tip to the sophist Protagoras, finally gets his epoch: in the absence of all horizons, man now is the measure of all things. And since "man" no longer has any fixed meaning—including biologically so—there is no fixed measure; and since there is no fixed measure, there is nothing left to decide moral and political questions but raw, toothy power: sometimes snarling, sometimes grinning, but always with eye on domination and never content in its newly acquired territory. Benedict again: "Man's destructive power has reached dimensions that can sometimes make us shudder."[3]

Jordan Peterson gets this. He, too, shudders, even as (or, perhaps, because) he stands up straight with his shoulders back. His *12 Rules for Life* is imbued with a haunting awareness, sometimes buried, sometimes surface, that the question of God remains *the* question—*the* moral question, *the* political question, even *the* psychological question—no matter how far we've technologically advanced beyond our first parents. Indeed, Peterson calls out those who claim to be atheists but who can't bring themselves to live like atheists. Addressing a hypothetical critic, he writes,

---

2. Ratzinger, *Christianity and the Crisis of Cultures*, 26.
3. Ratzinger, 25.

> You might object, "But I'm an atheist." No, you're *not*. . . . You're simply
> not an atheist in your actions, and it is your actions that most accurately
> reflect your deepest beliefs—those are that implicit, embedded in your
> being, underneath your conscious apprehension and articulable attitudes
> and surface-level self-knowledge. You can only find out what you actually
> believe (rather than what you think you believe) by watching how you
> act.[4]

Peterson sees that acting as if God does not exist—really acting that
way—doesn't offer an antidote to chaos. It embraces chaos, severed from
any conception of order. It is madness, but not the ironic "noble" madness
of Nietzsche's anti-hero in *The Madman and the Death of God*. It's the disheveled wild-eyed madness, the street-raving madness, the teeth-gnashing,
face-picking, howl-at-the-moon madness eviscerated of any cheeky sense of
"getting it out of one's system." It's the rejection of systems, the rejection
of normalcy, indeed, the rejection of rationality itself (the rejection of the
truth of rejection). This madness can never end well, because it cannot ever
progress or, properly speaking, even begin. Like the underground man of
Fyodor Dostoevsky (one of Peterson's favorite authors), embracing honest
atheism leaves you alone without even the solace of yourself. Peterson again:

> What has emerged [in the wake of the perishing of God] however—and
> this is an issue of central importance—is something even more dead; some-
> thing that was never alive, even in the past: *nihilism, as well as an equally
> dangerous susceptibility to new, totalizing utopian ideas*. . . . Nietzsche, for
> his part, posited that individual human beings would have to invent their
> own values in the aftermath of God's death. This is the element of his
> thinking that appears weakest, psychologically: *we cannot invent our own
> values, because we cannot merely impose what we believe on our souls*.[5]

---

4. Jordan B. Peterson, *12 Rules for Life: An Antidote to Chaos* (New York: Penguin Books, 2019), 103.

5. Peterson, 193.

God, in other words, is not dead for Jordan Peterson, even if he's not yet demonstrably alive. The chary psychologist and the prophetic pope thus stand on common ground: *All is not well in the kingdom*, and much of the contagion finds it source in a crisis of unbelief. Peterson thus takes on the mantel not only of psychologist, philosopher, and public intellectual for our times. He is also a theologian, and, if I may, a pretty bloody good one sometimes.

But how should we interpret Peterson's theology, and how can we make it accessible and fruitful for both those inside and outside (and walking the line between) Christianity? The first step is to define theology. That is no easy thing to do, especially for a theologian. But for the sake of simplicity, we can identify two fundamental definitions, distinct from each other but also intimately related. Perhaps the most widely recognized comes from St. Anslem of Canterbury, also known for his arguments seeking to prove God's existence. Anselm defines theology as *fides quaerens intellectum* or "faith seeking understanding." The definition's basic insight is that theological reasoning takes place within a tradition of revelation. A classic example is the doctrine of the Trinity. As the *Catechism of the Catholic Church* observes, "[God's] innermost Being as Holy Trinity is a mystery that is inaccessible to reason alone or even to Israel's faith before the Incarnation of God's Son and the sending of the Holy Spirit."[6] That God is one and three and three and one, and that the persons of the Holy Trinity can be identified as "Father," "Son," and "Holy Spirit," is a matter of revealed faith. Rational reflection can't figure that out on its own.

However, that does not mean that reason must remain idle in the reception or explanation of the doctrine. That's what Anselm means by "seeking understanding": the human mind can and should work within a given doctrine to clarify and deepen its meaning and application. Theologians take this task as a matter of profession, but anyone can do it—provided they're willing to accept the *a priori* truth of the doctrine, to work as "insiders" within the tradition.

---

6. *Catechism of the Catholic Church*, 237.

That's the first definition of theology. But there's another, more expansive definition, one that not only invites the theologian to think outside a tradition but also to think outside of thought itself. From this standpoint—the standpoint that seeks to transcend all standpoints—we might reformulate St. Anselm's motto as "understanding seeking understanding." This form of theology is not tradition bound per se. However, it still traffics within the horizon of some form of faith, some form of trust in that which cannot be directly known yet must be presumed for anything else to be known. How, for example, can we prove the validity of what Aristotle identified as the three laws of thought—the law of identity (a thing is what it is), the law of noncontradiction (a thing cannot both be itself and its opposite), and the law of the excluded middle (something either is or is not)? Thought and speech are impossible without these laws, yet we cannot explain why they are rational, why we have reason to believe in them, without using the very same laws. In other words, we can't get "beneath" them in an explanatory sense. So what other option do we have but to have faith in them, to trust in the conditions that make rationality itself possible?

But one could respond: Isn't that doing philosophy rather than theology? The distinctions can get academic at this point; yet, given that "theology" comes from the combination of the Greek words *theos* (meaning "God") and *logos* (meaning, among other things, "rationality" or "reason" itself), then doing theology minimally means reasoning about God, or expressed more expansively, reasoning about the biggest questions that we can possibly ask about existence. And while you may not have to affirm allegiance to a faith tradition in the strict sense to do theology this way (in the broad sense, everyone belongs to some intellectual tradition), answering these big questions, even tentatively, requires recognizing that having faith is embedded in the capacity to be able to think and reach conclusions at all. As St. John Paul II expresses this point in *Fides et Ratio* (*Faith and Reason*), "With the light of reason human beings can know which path to take, but they can follow that path to its end, quickly and unhindered, only if with a rightly tuned spirit they search for it within the horizon of faith."[7]

---

7. Pope John Paul II, *Fides et Ratio*, 16, encyclical letter, Vatican website, September 14, 1998, http://www.vatican.va/content/john-paul-ii/en/encyclicals/documents/hf_jp-ii_enc_14091998_fides-et-ratio.html.

12 Rules for Life engages in both forms of theology. The questions Peterson addresses—questions about order, chaos, meaning, and purpose both in and of themselves and in relation to human life—fall squarely in the broader sense of theology, especially given his frequent appeals to God, transcendence, and, his favorite word, "Being." Each rule, individually and in relation to the others, is grounded in a metaphysical inquiry, both implicitly and explicitly, about the nature of existence as such.

However, Peterson also has a foot within the Christian tradition, especially its adoption of Old Testament creation and fall narratives. To be sure, he employs Christian ideas to make broader psychological and moral points to non-Christian audiences. Yet at the same time, he can also sound like an insider, coy enough to generate doubt about whether he's *really* a believer, but writing with a prophetic tone that makes one think, "How could he say this and *not* believe?" One possibly revelatory moment, among many, occurs under rule number three. He writes,

> [Jesus'] Sermon on the Mount outlines the true nature of man, and the proper aim of mankind: concentrate on the day, so that you can live in the present, and attend completely and properly to what is right in front of you—but do that only after you have decided to let what is within you shine forth, so that it can justify Being and illuminate the world.[8]

Would that the faithful could hear more messages like this!

Caution, though, is also in order; I don't want to overplay my hand on this point. Peterson repeatedly asks his readers to cast away "low-resolution" views of reality. It is excellent advice. Things are complicated. People, more so. Peterson, even more than that. If there's ever been a public intellectual who can appeal to so many different kinds of people without showing his cards (or showing his cards in a way that is too complex to categorize), it's Peterson. He certainly sounds like a Christian at times. But he can also sound

---

8. Peterson, *12 Rules for Life,* 109–110.

like a Stoic, a Taoist, a Gnostic Manichean, a Jungian (especially a Jungian), a Kantian, a Platonist, an evolutionary biologist with an interest in ethics, a Humean virtue theorist, and a mild devotee of Nietzsche. Among others. That makes him a hard square to circle. Nevertheless, there remains a there there in Peterson's theology, both in the broad and specific senses—and, as he might say, that's not nothing. He may not be in the Church, in other words, but it's fair to say he's somewhere in the vicinity. For that reason, his thought is worth engaging in greater depth both for Christians and for all those willing to take Christianity seriously.

That's what the chapters in this section seek to do, to mine Peterson's two forms of theology with three goals in mind: 1) understanding Peterson, 2) learning from Peterson, and 3) critiquing Peterson with an evangelical eye—meaning seeking to show how Christian orthodoxy, what C.S. Lewis called "mere Christianity," provides a more comprehensive and accurate accounting of, and solution to, the problems Peterson so brilliantly diagnoses. Accomplishing these goals requires reorganizing the 12 rules along thematic lines:

1. **The Problem of Meaning and Its Pursuit:** Pursue What Is Meaningful and Stand Up Straight with Your Shoulders Back (rules seven and one)

2. **The Problem of Pride and Its Antidote:** Tell the Truth or at Least Don't Lie; Be Precise in Your Speech; and Assume the Person You Are Listening to Might Know Something You Don't Know (rules eight, nine, and ten)

3. **The Problem of True Love:** Treat Yourself Like Someone You Are Responsible for Helping; Do Not Let Your Children Do Anything That Makes You Dislike Them; and Make Friends with People Who Want the Best for You (rules two, three, and five)

4. **The Problem of Creation and Redemption:** Compare Yourself to Who You Were Yesterday, Not to Who Someone Else Is Today; Set Your House in Perfect Order Before You Change the World; Don't Bother Children When They Are Skateboarding; and Pet a Cat When You Encounter One on the Street (rules four, six, eleven, and twelve)

The aim of this analysis is to persuade two audiences of two things: 1) Christians have good reason to engage Peterson as a fruitful theological and moral resource and, indeed, ally; 2) non-Christian admirers of Peterson have good reason to consider that his ideas might make the most sense when refined within a Christian theological horizon.

In short, Peterson makes a superb case for living *as if* God exists. But there's an even better one to be made for living *given* that God exists.

CHAPTER 7

The Problem of Meaning and Its Pursuit

One of the dogmas of secularity is that we can make a clean cut between "fact" and "value." The division serves both a philosophical and practical purpose for the dogma's adherents, one that permits society to segregate "public" questions of policy from "personal" beliefs in the domain of morality and religion. This view's anthem includes the refrain, "I have my truth, you have yours," and the dispositive, one-size-fits-all rebuttal, "That's just *your* opinion." Excluding the most radical, who, fortunately, are sequestered in universities, most do not take this distinction to mean there is no such thing as "truth" per se, only moral and religious truth. There are still the "hard sciences" to provide us the facts, which, in turn, provide the basis for a shared epistemic and social reality.

This is a tempting template for individual and communal life. Each of us gets to believe whatever we want about the meaning of existence while still thinking ourselves civilized because we defer to a priestly class of experts who examine the entrails of existence and tell us what's really real when necessary. But Peterson, one of the experts himself, knows better. Fact and value are inseparable for him in two fundamental ways: 1) values structure how we perceive anything at all, including "facts," and 2) how we structure our actions, individually and communally, cannot be determined simply by "fact" or simply by "values."

One of the foundational pieces of Peterson's epistemology, his view of how we know what we know, is that our vision is shaped and delimited by our will. In other words, what we want (or think we want) determines what we perceive. As Peterson puts it, "What you aim at determines what you see."[1] There are biological reason for this. Sight, observes Peterson, is "expensive," meaning it consumes lots of brain power. Humans thus naturally focus on the bits of reality that maximize getting what they want. This also applies to vision in a more comprehensive sense, how, for example, we "see" ourselves, others, and what defines "the world." These phenomena do not appear naked in and of themselves (what Immanuel Kant would call "noumena"); rather, they are *filtered* through the lens of our desires, both conscious and unconscious. As Peterson explains, "The world reveals itself to us as something to utilize and something to navigate through—not as something that merely is."[2] Put differently, there is no such thing as valueless fact. Or, if there is, *we* can't see it.

This observation points to the second pole of Peterson's epistemology, which also illuminates his broader understanding of human nature: given that acting in a particular way depends on our vision (what we see), and what we see depends upon what we value, our actions are always rooted in both the perception and pursuit of value. In other words, a) there's no such thing as a "neutral" or "value-free" action, and b) we always act in pursuit of meaning connected to a specific goal. As Peterson puts it, "In the absence of . . . a system of value, people simply cannot act. In fact, they can't even perceive, because both action and perception require a goal, and a valid goal is, by necessity, something valued."[3] This claim, for Peterson, is a truism. How could we understand action if not tied to pursuing a goal? And how could we think of what it means to have a goal but to accept that we perceive the goal to be valuable? Yet he also points to a complication in this relationship between vision, action, and value: human beings frequently desire incompatibly different things. He writes,

> We can't just get the one particular thing we especially want now, along with everything else we usually want, because our desires can produce conflict with our other desires, as well as with other people and with the

---

1. Jordan B. Peterson, *12 Rules for Life: An Antidote to Chaos* (New York: Penguin Books, 2019), 96.
2. Peterson, 261.
3. Peterson, xxxi.

world. Thus we must become conscious of our desires, and articulate them, and prioritize them, and arrange them into *hierarchies*.[4]

Peterson recognizes, moreover, that there ultimately must be one goal, one purpose, that organizes all our desires into a coherent hierarchy that, in turn, makes action possible. He calls this goal the "meta-goal," arguing, "All such concrete goals can and should be subordinated to what might be considered a meta goal, which is a way of approaching and formulating goals themselves."[5] This meta-goal is the *one* purpose that orients all our other proximate goals and makes choosing among incommensurate aims (e.g., earning more money vs. spending more time with your family) possible. Failure to have a meta-goal is to risk entering a state of paralysis the first time you find yourself wanting two opposing things at the same time.

However, it's one thing to recognize that all action is value-imbued and goal-oriented and that there must be one goal toward which all our actions aim. But even if that is true, we are still left with the most important question: *What defines—or should define—our meta-goal?* This is the primary question Peterson addresses in rule seven, "Pursue what is meaningful, not what is expedient." The difference between "expedience" and "meaning" hinges on the willingness to sacrifice for what Peterson calls "the betterment of Being," a goal that includes alleviating unnecessary suffering and diminishing moral evil. Meaning defined this way takes the form of a Kantian-like maxim that governs all action. As Peterson puts it, "Make [it] an axiom: to the best of my ability I will act in a manner that leads to the alleviation of unnecessary pain and suffering."[6]

Crucially, Peterson attributes an either/or character to this maxim and employs biblical language to drive home his point: working for the betterment of Being puts you on the side of Christ. Living for yourself, on the other hand, puts you in league with the devil. As he explains,

4. Peterson, 101–102 (emphasis added).
5. Peterson, 226–227.
6. Peterson, 198.

It's Abel or Cain—and it's Christ or Satan. If it's working for the ennobling of Being, for the establishment of Paradise, then it's Christ. If it's working for the destruction of Being, for the generation of unnecessary suffering and pain, then it's Satan. That's the inescapable, archetypal reality.[7]

To reject expedience, to be on the side of Christ, necessarily involves sacrifice, embracing suffering (which does not mean pursuing it) for the sake of reducing it in the world. In contrast, a satanic orientation seduces you into aiming exclusively for your own self-interest, rejecting sacrifice and acting according to the maxim "look out only for number one." It's a recipe for living an individual and collective hell, not least because we frequently misperceive what is in our true self-interest. As Peterson writes, "To have meaning in your life is better than to have what you want, because you may neither know what you want, nor what you truly need."[8]

Two Loves, One God

How can we assess this remarkable proposal from someone who will not commit to believing in God yet exhorts everyone to choose Christ over Satan? The first thing to say is that he's right, both formally and (though Peterson may not agree) substantively. By saying he's formally right, I mean Peterson accurately captures the nature of, and relationship between, perception, action, and the necessity of a meta-goal. Independently of whatever substance we might attribute to an individual's particular conception of meaning, it appears true that no one can a) completely sever fact from value or b) act independently of a value hierarchy. The perception of value is, as Peterson argues, inherent in the act of perception itself, a feature of human knowing that becomes visible the moment we ask, "Why am I looking at this rather than that?" The answer—whatever the "this" or "that" may be—always points to some goal we have in mind, implicitly or explicitly. This would also

---

7. Peterson, 199.
8. Peterson, 200.

include having the goal of "objectivity"; in saying, "I want to see this thing, this event, this person objectively," I am saying, "I have the goal of seeing this object as it truly is." That doesn't mean that we look at everything we do because we desire it. Indeed, the opposite might be the case: we might be looking at something or someone because we perceive a threat and are deliberating whether to fight or flee. Either way, Peterson's point stands: the aim that we have in mind always influences, if not determines, what we see.

This aim, moreover, is not only necessarily tied to value. It's necessarily tied to a hierarchy of values, a truth that emerges the moment two or more mutually exclusive goals compete for your allegiance: for example, wanting to spend more time with your family and more time at work, eating whatever you want while having good health, being faithful in your marriage and wanting sexual freedom. To settle these internal disputes, a "higher" goal must intervene that renders one aim more valuable than the other.[9] That "higher" aim, in turn, must be governed by an even higher one, which, eventually, reaches its culmination in a meta-goal. The aim-chain, in other words, cannot go on forever; at some point you must recognize that there is one goal that orders every other goal you have, a goal that serves as an end point for your action, one that permits you to say, "I aim to do this for its own sake," rather than "I do this in order that I can do something else." That goal is not only singular—it's one thing—it is also comprehensive, and choosing it means we are not choosing its opposite.

I think Peterson's formally right about all of this. But is he also right substantively about the fact that the meta-goal is ultimately a choice between God and Satan? I think he is, but perhaps in a way that Peterson himself does not articulate. To see why, it's important to recognize that Peterson's argument, as original as it may sound to secular ears, is echoing

---

9. Someone could respond that the way they settle conflicting goals is to pursue the goal that reflects their *strongest* desire. However, that goal, in turn, would generate the question: What is the *goal* of always following my strongest desire? What it is about "intensity" of desire that I find most valuable in terms of adjudicating my actions? Following one's strongest desires, in other words, does not extricate someone from the question of the hierarchy of values. Moreover, it's probably not a good recipe for a happy life: How often would you get out of bed in the morning if your highest goal in life were to follow your *strongest* desire, whatever it may be?

fundamental insights from Christian theological anthropology, especially as
those doctrines take shape in the thought of St. Augustine (354–430) and St.
Thomas Aquinas (1224–1274). Although Peterson does not cite Augustine or
Aquinas in *12 Rules*, the ancient Christian thinkers and the contemporary
psychologist converge on the same insight about the importance of having
an ultimate aim in life.

St. Augustine, for example, conceived of the problem of human existence, a "problem" only because we chose to fall from our natural perfection,
in terms of a choice, an either/or, between two loves: the love of God (*caritas*)
or the love of something other than God (*cupiditas*). The choice between
God and not-God does not apply to proximate objects of love—for example
loving one's spouse, loving one's job, loving one's car—but rather to the final
object of love, what one loves beyond all else, or, put in Peterson's language,
the meta-goal of your love. In this respect, Augustine argues, we either love
God as the ultimate object of our love or we don't; and if we don't, we are
by definition engaged in idolatry, loving something other than God as if it
were our God. This is a theme throughout Augustine's vast corpus, but he
formulates it pithily in his description of the "City of God" and the "City of
Man":

> Accordingly, two cities have been formed by two loves: the earthly by the
> love of self, even to the contempt of God; the heavenly by the love of God,
> even to the contempt of self. The former, in a word, glories in itself, the
> latter in the Lord. For the one seeks glory from men; but the greatest glory
> of the other is God, the witness of conscience. The one lifts up its head in
> its own glory; the other says to its God, "You are my glory and the lifter
> up of my head." In the one, the princes and the nations it subdues are
> ruled by the love of ruling; in the other, the princes and the subjects serve
> one another in love, the latter obeying, while the former take thought for
> all. The one delights in its own strength, represented in the persons of its
> rulers; the other says to its God, "I will love You, O Lord, my strength."[10]

---

10. Augustine, *City of God* 14.28.

These loves, for Augustine, not only determine how we act in relation to ourselves and to others. They determine how *we see* ourselves and others, as well. To love God is to see things as they really are, as they really exist; to love something other than God, in contrast, is to see it through the filter of pride, arrogance, and, in Peterson's language, expedience. As Augustine argues in his dialogue, *The Teacher,*

> [The truth is that which] every rational soul does indeed consult, but it reveals itself to each according to his capacity to grasp it by reason of the good or evil dispositions of his will. . . . If the soul is sometimes mistaken, this does not come about because of any defect on the part of the truth it consulted, just as it is not through any defect in the light outside us that our bodily eyes are often deceived.[11]

What we will, in other words, determines what we see. Thus, if our will is bad—if our aim is bad—then we will not see what is true, what is real. That bad vision, in turn, prompts us to act badly, which, in turn, generates a vicious circle of bad action that, eventually, leads us to become a bad person. Happily, the opposite is also true: aiming at the truth, willing the true good, empowers you to see the truth, which, in turn, not only prompts you to act on its behalf but also to become the kind of person who does so naturally—that is, to be a good person. Since God is the only perfect good, the only fully true truth (truth in and of itself), the only way, therefore, that we can see things as they really are and act accordingly, is to aim for God. Aiming for anything other than God is, consequently, to live a lie and, eventually, to imitate the father of lies himself, Satan.

In short, Augustine, like Peterson, offers human beings an either/or dichotomy to structure their lives: *either* live for God in the City of God (who,

---

11. Augustine, *De Magistro* (*The Teacher*) 38, in *The Teacher, The Free Choice of the Will, Grace and Free Will,* trans. Robert P. Russell (Washington, DC: The Catholic University of America Press, 2004), 51.

for him, is also Christ) *or* live for Satan in the City of Man. Translated into Peterson's language, either give your life to the only reality that is meaningful in and of itself or live according to your own self-interest.

Happiness: The Goal Beyond Which There Is No Other

There is a similar argument in the thought of the great medieval theologian, St. Thomas Aquinas. Aquinas devotes an extended section of his masterwork, the *Summa theologiae*, to defining happiness and the means by which human beings attain happiness. Authentic happiness and that which is "meaningful" is one and the same for him and, like Peterson,[12] Aquinas believes authentic meaning is an either/or proposition: God or nothing.

To start his analysis, Aquinas recognizes that human beings always act for a goal; in other words, what motivates everything that we do voluntarily is the attainment of some good that we have in mind. So, for example, a student goes to class because she wants participation points. However, Aquinas also notices that every goal we pursue in every action is, in fact, a subsidiary goal to a "higher," more overarching goal—so, for example, the student wants participation points because she wants to get a good grade in the class. But, of course, it doesn't stop there: the good grade is in service of wanting a high GPA, which is in service of becoming valedictorian, which is in service of attaining a good job, which is in service of securing a high income, which is in service of buying a nice home and car, which is in service of yet a higher goal. However, this chain of goals cannot go on indefinitely. There must be one final goal that organizes and motivates all of our other goals. In other words, whatever we do, Aquinas argues, we can ultimately trace it to one final goal (what Peterson calls a meta-goal) that both explains every other action

---

12. It is important to note that Peterson's use of "happiness," when he does use the word, is different from Aquinas' conception of happiness. Peterson seems to think of happiness qua happiness as the experience of good feelings. Happiness for Aquinas, on the other hand, is in the tradition of the Greek *eudaimonia,* meaning a comprehensive understanding of what it means to live a fully good, flourishing life. Peterson's conception of "meaning" is much closer to this understanding of happiness. Thus, when I refer to Peterson's conception of happiness in this context, I am specifically referring to his broader conception of meaning—not the mere presence of good feelings.

we have taken along the way and why we chose one subordinate goal over another when they conflicted (e.g., to draw on an example above, choosing to spend more time with your family rather than making more money). As Aquinas writes, "It is therefore necessary for the last end [i.e., goal] so to fill man's appetite that nothing is left besides it for man to desire."[13]

That highest goal, Aquinas argues—the goal in which all our desires finally come to rest—is what we call "happiness," and every human being, he observes, desires happiness. As with Peterson, the next logical question thus takes the form of how we should define the content of "happiness." Aquinas considers some possible options, including 1) money, 2) having a good reputation, 3) being famous, 4) being powerful, 5) having good health, and 6) experiencing pleasure. While each of these constitutes *a* good for Aquinas, none can serve as a final goal for human life, which is the same as saying none can make you happy. Money fails because wealth is only valuable insofar as it can buy you things and experiences and is, thus, by definition, only instrumental to happiness, not happiness itself. Having a good reputation can't be the highest good because attaining it is almost entirely out of our hands (think, for example, of a good person who has been slandered) and something that you can never possess because there is always more of it to pursue. Being famous can't be the highest good for the same reasons, and we also have to add that you can be famous for being evil (for example, which name do you think the world will still remember in a hundred years: Justin Bieber or Adolf Hitler?). Defining power as the highest good runs into the same problems: there is always more power you could possibly attain, meaning you can never actually possess it. Moreover, power itself is a neutral tool (like money) that can be used for good or evil. Good health is, of course, good, but it is similar to having money: it is only good insofar as it permits you to pursue other goals. It is possible to be in great health but also be miserably unhappy. Finally, pleasure doesn't work because it is still a good that we can never attain as a final goal because it is fleeting in nature, the desire for it is insatiable, and

---

13. Thomas Aquinas, *Summa theologiae* 1-2.1.5.

the pleasures of the body that a dog or cat could enjoy do not fully satisfy the distinctly human desires for understanding the truth and loving the good.

For Aquinas, the upshot of this argument is that nothing in the material world, nothing "created," as he calls it, can offer humans authentic happiness, which, in turn, generates a predicament: humans cannot *not* act for a final end, cannot *not* seek happiness; however, nothing in the world can offer that which human beings long for. The solution to this problem is thus to accept that authentic happiness is possible only if we choose to live for that which is transcendently "outside" the material world and, indeed, that which makes the material world possible: God. Aquinas again:

> It is impossible for any created good to constitute man's happiness. For happiness is the perfect good, which satisfies the appetite altogether; else it would not be the last end, if something yet remained to be desired. . . . Hence it is evident that nothing can satisfy man's will save the universal good. This is to be found, not in any creature, but in God alone; because every creature has goodness by participation. Wherefore God alone can satisfy the will of man, according to the words of the Psalm 102:5: "Who satisfies your desire with good things.[14]

Either aim for God and live a meaningful and authentically happy existence or live for something other than God, other than truth and goodness itself, and slip into meaninglessness. The latter choice, Aquinas makes clear, is not only false in the sense of being contrary to the nature of reality. It is also, and consequently, a formula for being perpetually frustrated, perpetually empty, perpetually drawn back into yourself, and perpetually separated from the source of existence itself—which is to say, in the absence of God. *Hell,* in other words. Thus, as with Augustine, Aquinas offers us two choices and only two choices for life: Christ or Satan.

---

14. Thomas Aquinas, 1-2.2.8.

Onward "Christian" Soldiers?

This foray into two great theological minds hopefully shows that Peterson's conception of meaning finds deep resonance, if not overlap, in fundamental Christian doctrines. But so what? Why can't we just say that Peterson happens to agree with some things some Christian theists have said and leave it at that? We don't need a *real* God, a *real* Christ, to make Peterson's argument work. Do we?

Yes. We do. As much as Peterson may agree with the *language* of Augustine and Aquinas, he leaves whether "Christ" and "Satan" pertain to ontological realities (meaning, they really exist) ambiguous. Indeed, his argument indicates that "Christ" is merely a symbolic placeholder—not the historical Jesus Christ, God's only Son, whom Christians believe was conceived by the Holy Spirit, suffered under Pontius Pilate, was crucified, died, and buried, and rose on the third day. The same goes for Satan, though on the opposite side of the semiotic spectrum. As he writes,

> Mary's son, Christ, offers Himself to God and the world, to betrayal, to torture and death—to the very point of despair on the cross, where he cries out those terrible words: *my God, my God, why hast though forsaken me?* (Matt. 27:46). That is the *archetypal* story of the man who gives his all for the sake of the better—who offers up his life for the advancement of Being—who allows God's will to become manifest fully within the confines of a single life. That is the model for the honorable man.[15]

"Archetypal" sticks out here. What does that mean? Setting aside how deeply Peterson has been influenced by Carl Jung, whose psychological analysis draws deeply on archetypes, this is the fundamental question: Does saying Christ is "archetypal" mean that Christ ontologically *is* the model for "honorable" (i.e., meaningful) existence? Or does it mean he *represents* a

---

15. Peterson, *12 Rules for Life*, 171 (emphasis added on *archetypal*).

model for such a life? In other word, is Christ God or not? Or, more broadly: is God God, or not?

I do not know how Peterson would answer this question. His use of archetypes is slippery, perhaps in deference to the complexity of existence, but slippery, nonetheless. But let's say that archetype means the latter, that Christ is, ultimately, only a *symbol* of a pragmatic truth that human (sub) consciousness has conjured over millions of years of evolution as a way to survive a hostile world. *If* that's the case, Peterson's conception of meaning begins to lose meaning.

Why? Peterson is clear that living for his conception of Christ is not easy; it requires sacrifice, the greatest of sacrifice, even. Indeed, that is what distinguishes meaning from expedience: expedience is to live without sacrifice (and to lose everything), while meaning is to embrace sacrifice (and to gain everything). Yet to sacrifice in the name of a symbol, a symbol disconnected from a transcendent reality, raises two interrelated problems, one epistemic and the other motivational. First, if the highest good is merely a symbol, then how do I know that which I am living for has any substantive content? How do I know that it is not, ultimately, a void, a nullity, an absence, a sheer invention of an anxious mind? Second, if I can't know what I'm living for, then, put bluntly, why would I live for it, much less sacrifice for it?

Peterson would likely offer a pragmatic response to these questions: "Well, we might not be able to know whether or that Christ is, but we sure as hell know that the alternative is hell." Indeed, he says as much in his discussion of the meaning of meaning, suggesting, in utilitarian terms, that the reason you sacrifice, the reason you choose "Christ" over "Satan," is to avoid greater suffering, both individually and communally. As he writes,

[Living for Christ places] at the pinnacle of your moral hierarchy a set of presuppositions and actions aimed at the betterment of Being. Why? Because we know the alternative. The alternative was the 20th century. The alternative was so close to Hell that the difference is not worth discussing.[16]

---

16. Peterson, 198.

The goal, moreover, is not only to avoid "hell"; it's to get the best lot out of life, to be as happy as possible in an existence defined by suffering. Observing the general human tendency to offer sacrifices, Peterson observes that "[humans] thought it over and drew a conclusion: *The successful among us delay gratification. The successful among us bargain with the future.*"[17]

So sacrifice in the pursuit of meaning is what leads to a "successful" life, or, at least, the most successful life possible. But what problem has this solved if goodness isn't real, if Christ, the incarnation of goodness, isn't real? This is the issue. If there is no ontological or even rational content to the existence of absolute goodness, then everything else in the system of meaning breaks down because its foundation, its touchstone, dissolves into sand. To live a meaningful life, according to Peterson, is to live to diminish suffering. Yet defining "suffering," giving it content, requires defining the good that suffering violates. It seems, however, that Peterson's argument ultimately offers this circular response: "The good is overcoming suffering to the extent that it is possible in human life, and what it means to overcome suffering is to pursue what is good (what is meaningful) no matter what."

This may sound like academic nitpicking, trafficking in an abstraction in the face of something whose meaning everyone understands. But establishing fixed content for the definition of the highest good, the meta-goal, is not pedantic. *It is necessary to establish the difference between "expedience" and "meaning" in the first place.* The tyrants of the twentieth century, and every previous century, believed they were following Peterson's maxim, acting so as to diminish unnecessary suffering in the world. Hitler and Stalin had an ultimate goal. Both of them sought world domination via National Socialism for Hitler or International Socialism for Stalin. The problem wasn't that they didn't have a meta-goal, in other words. The problem is that they had a false meta-goal, which generated a false perception of the world and a false definition of suffering and its remedy. Even if we say they

---

17. Peterson, 169.

misperceived the good because their aim was wrong, which is no doubt the case, that only points back to the need for a fixed definition of the highest good. And saying the highest good is overcoming suffering, in turn, just resets the cycle.

Put differently, the meaningfulness of suffering is determined by the goal that is pursued. But absent a goal that is truly worth pursuing, our suffering cannot have redemptive value. It is one thing to suffer in the service of a great cause like liberating Europe from Nazi tyranny, but to suffer for a triviality is torture.

That, in short, is the problem of appealing to symbols, to archetypes with no content, to define the meaning of meaning. If there is no substantively, as opposed to pragmatically, true content to what defines the good, then everyone, without exception, lives according to their own self-interest alone because there is no alternative. In this case, agreement on what defines the good, to the extent that it exists, is accidental. What Immanuel Kant calls hypothetical imperatives, acting in the name of the "good" so long as it serves your self-interest, would be possible. But categorical imperatives—acting in the name of the good no matter what—would be impossible because "the good," having neither metaphysical nor rational content, would have no authority to compel and even less to persuade. The consequence is that both Christ and Satan would dissipate in the amoral wash. Even the Father of Lies can't speak when there is no truth.[18]

---

18. An example may help illustrate the stakes here. If "meaning" has no objective truth, then people can define it however they want to. Sometimes those definitions might accidently overlap, for example, in people who "agree" that it is wrong to sell drugs to children. However, one person may think it is wrong because she personally believes that it is immoral to cause harm to children, while the other person may think it is wrong because he personally believes it's immoral (i.e., against his self-interest) to get caught and go to jail. The latter person has what Immanuel Kant calls a "hypothetical imperative": he believes he shouldn't do something "wrong" *only so long* as he thinks there might be negative consequences (that is, consequences he doesn't like) if he does it. The former person, on the other hand, has what is called a "categorical imperative": she thinks she shouldn't do bad things *no matter what*, whatever the consequences of the action might be. The point is that if there is no objective truth, then there are no categorical imperatives because the definition of truth *only* depends on each person's definition of what they think is right. Using the same example, the first person would never sell drugs to children, while the second would do so the moment he had sufficient reason to believe he wouldn't be caught. Which one of them is acting morally? If there is no truth, the answer is: both.

Stand Up Straight or Whatever

This all has implications for Peterson's conception of courage, which he lays out in the first chapter, "Stand up straight with your shoulders back." Drawing on evolutionary biology, Peterson argues that those who stand strong in the face of life's many dangers, those who refuse to cower in the face of a threat, do much better in every empirical category of well-being than the alternative, those who, like a defeated lobster, slip into the first crevice they find at even the whiff of confrontation. Being courageous benefits both the individual and the community in this sense. As Peterson writes, "If you say no, early in the cycle of oppression, and you mean what you say (which means you state your refusal in no uncertain terms and stand behind it) then the scope for oppression will remain properly bounded and limited." He continues, "It is in this manner that the willingness of the individual to stand up for him- or herself protects everyone from the corruption of society."[19]

Here, again, Peterson links right action to good outcomes in a utilitarian sense. He is clear that standing up for yourself will involve pain, but equally clear that the alternative is more pain, for yourself and everyone else. Being courageous, therefore, is a prerequisite for pursuing authentic meaning in life. As he explains,

> To stand up straight with your shoulders back is to accept the terrible responsibility of life, with eyes wide open. It means deciding to voluntarily transform the chaos of potential into the realities of habitable order . . . it means willingly undertaking the sacrifices necessary to generate a productive and meaningful reality (it means acting like God, in the ancient language).[20]

Peterson understands that courage is a morally neutral trait by itself; it needs a morally good purpose to render it virtuous (think, for example, of the

---

19. Peterson, 24.
20. Peterson, 27.

courageous Nazi). That purpose, for him, as we see in the above passage, is to "please God," which is the same as choosing Christ over Satan.

This, however, only returns us to square one. If courage needs a purpose to give it morally good content, and we identify that content as a symbol that, itself, is ultimately vacuous ("Being" disconnected from something *real*), then all we end up doing is pulling the rug from beneath courage itself, both epistemologically and motivationally. Put bluntly, why would we fight for something we cannot define?

Peterson would probably reply, drawing again on evolutionary biology (the lobsters), that the alternative is worse, resulting in lower serotonin levels and lower social outcomes like unemployment and unstable relationships. There remain two problems, however: 1) saying some outcomes are worse than others *begs* the most important question, which is still at issue: *Good and bad outcomes according to what standard of the good?*, and 2) absent a fixed standard of the good—relying, for example, on serotonin levels alone—why wouldn't we say that living a meaningful life means maximizing serotonin, which, in turn means becoming as powerful as possible, like dominant lobsters? If that's the case, how then do we differentiate between the rush from being a bully from the rush to standing up to a bully? How do we differentiate between heroes and villains? Both exhibit a kind of courage.

For Augustine and Aquinas, in contrast, real courage is in service of the goals of love. We cannot love without courage. When the difficulties of life inevitably arise, and they will, we will lack the strength and toughness to continue. Without courage, we will only love on sunny days, but when the storms of life come, we will retreat and give up. For Augustine and Aquinas, the villain can, at best, exhibit a kind of fake courage that is "tough" but for no particular end. This "courage" is not a true virtue because true virtue is what leads to authentic meaning in life—namely, a life full of love for God and neighbor.

Ultimately, it's not clear how Peterson's argument can make this distinction between real courage and fake courage, between desire for any goal versus desiring a goal that is worth desiring. Consequently, it's also not clear how he can offer a culture hungry for authentic heroes a consistent and durable reason for *why* they should fight on the side of the good. For if there's no transcendent good, you might as well be a villain. Or better yet, a hidden spectator to someone else's battle, creeping among the rubble and scavenging the leftovers.

Keep Reading

Peterson's account of meaning and its pursuit is timely, intellectually rich, and ennobling (the most recurrent thought I have reading his work is: "Man, I have to get my life together like *this* guy"). But it needs a theological foundation and a theological horizon to make it work, both philosophically, in terms of its internal consistency, and psychologically, in terms of its power to persuade and motivate.

Thus, in the end, if you think Peterson's onto something important in rules seven and one—and I think he certainly is—may I suggest two additional authors to read: St. Augustine and St. Thomas Aquinas.[21] Both agree with Peterson's basic proposal but would add that the symbol of the good as your meta-goal makes the most sense only when it is grounded in a real man, and when that man, in turn, is grounded in the real God. This, they believe, is true, but it is also pragmatic: if sacrifice is necessary to live a meaningful life, we had better give people more than an archetype to live—and die—for.

---

21. For an introduction, see James K.A. Smith, *On the Road with St. Augustine: A Real-World Spirituality for Restless Hearts* (Grand Rapids, MI: Brazos, 2019) and Ralph McInerny, *Ethica Thomistica, Revised Edition: The Moral Philosophy of Thomas Aquinas* (Washington, DC: The Catholic University of America Press, 1997).

CHAPTER 8

The Problem of Pride and Its Antidote

At first blush, Jordan Peterson's rule to tell the truth appears to rest on utilitarian grounds, like what we saw in the previous chapter. One of his longstanding research interests is how monstrous men like Hitler in Germany, Stalin in Russia, Pol Pot in Cambodia (and, we might add, Kim Jong-il in North Korea) can come to power and extinguish so many lives. One explanation, Peterson observes, is the human proclivity to tell little lies that, over time, inure individuals to the arrival of the Big Lie. As Peterson writes, drawing on the work of the psychiatrist and concentration-camp survivor Viktor Frankl, *"deceitful, inauthentic individual existence is the precursor to social totalitarianism."*[1] He adds,

> What you see of a lie when you act it out (and most lies are acted out, rather than told) is very little of what actually is. A lie is connected to everything else. It produces the same effect on the world that a single drop of sewage produces in even the largest crystal magnum of champagne. It is something best considered living and growing. . . . When the lies get big enough, the world spoils. . . . Lies corrupt the world. Worse, that is their intent.[2]

The reason we should tell the truth, therefore, is to prevent individual and social destruction. The more we lie, the more we suffer. Thus, to lie less is to suffer less.

---

1. Jordan B. Peterson, *12 Rules for Life: An Antidote to Chaos* (New York: Penguin Books, 2019), 215.
2. Peterson, 228–229.

This is a compelling observation, no doubt accurate. However, taken by itself, the observation that lies lead to suffering returns to the problem of how to attribute stable content to "the good" so that we might have a stable definition for "suffering," especially since telling the truth inevitably leads to suffering as well. We need to know what is authentically good, what is ultimately true, to understand both what it is to tell the truth and why we should always do so (or at least not lie). The critique from the previous chapter applies here as well.

Nevertheless, Peterson's analysis contains insight into a related problem that is as important as truth-telling itself: the human capacity to idolize, in the sense of turn into a false god, human reason itself. As he writes,

> Reason falls in love with itself, and worse. It falls in love with its own productions. It elevates them, and worships them as absolutes. . . . It is the greatest temptation of the rational faculty to glorify its own capacity and its own productions and to claim that in the face of its theories nothing transcendent or outside its domain need exist.[3]

Believing in the absoluteness of reason, Peterson points out, is akin to a lie and, like all lies, leads to totalitarianism if left unchecked. Indeed, he argues that the absolutizing of reason is itself a form of totalitarianism, writing, "That is what *totalitarianism* means: Everything that needs to be discovered has been discovered."[4] In addition to generating oppressive political realities, the idolatry of reason points to the greater *individual* tendency to be prideful, to claim to know more than I know, *to be* more than I am, and, in doing so, to re-create myself as my own object of worship. Peterson again: "The faculty of rationality inclines dangerously to pride: *all I know is all that needs to be known.* Pride falls in love with its own creations, and tries to make them absolute."[5]

---

3. Peterson, 218.
4. Peterson, 218.
5. Peterson, 210.

What, then, is the antidote to pride, especially given how dangerous it is to individual and social life? Peterson offers two responses: 1) be precise in your speech (rule ten), and 2) assume the person you are listening to might know something you don't (rule nine). Peterson draws much of the evidence in support of precise speech from his clinical experience. He observes, for example, that a necessary condition for effectively addressing a problem—in a marriage, with a boss, with a family member, even with oneself—is to define it with the most precision possible. Otherwise, individuals end up engulfed in chaos, drowned by every problem in life agglomerating into an amorphous mass of indistinguishable suffering. In this sense, defining the problem properly, isolating it from everything else, is the first step to fixing it, or at least diminishing the suffering associated with it. As Peterson explains,

> If you identify things, with careful attention and language, you bring them forward as viable, obedient objects, detaching them from their underlying near-universal connectedness. You simplify them. You make them specific and useful, and reduce their complexity. You make it possible to live with them and use them without dying from that complexity, with its attendant and uncertain anxiety.[6]

On the surface, this might merely sound like good advice for conflict resolution. However, precision in speech also points directly back to the problem of pride and its antidote: disciplining your speech, doing everything possible to describe things specifically, helps protect you from drifting into the totalizing tendency of the idolatry of reason and the accompanying conceit that one already knows all there is to know. As Peterson explains,

> When we look at the world, we perceive only what is enough for our plans and actions to work and for us to get by. . . . That is radical, functional, unconscious simplification of the world—and it's almost impossible for us not to mistake it for the world itself. But the objects we see are not simply

---

6. Peterson, 281.

there, in the world, for our simple, direct perceiving . . . . *It is for this reason that we must be precise in our aim.*[7]

Precision, in other words, is an essential condition for right perception. Specificity gets us closer to the way things actually are, closer to the truth. The opposite—what Peterson calls "low resolution" vision—has the opposite effect, moving us deeper into selfish desires, what we *want* the world to be, and hence, further from the way the world is, further from the truth. In this sense, precision helps keep us humble, and humility is the enemy of pride.

Peterson's ninth rule serves a similar purpose. Though much of the chapter offers practical advice on how to listen authentically and how to speak to different audiences, there is a deeper principle of humility here as well.[8] Speaking to the "everyman," Peterson observes,

> There is a mysterious arbitrariness about [how you perceive yourself and your memories]. You don't form a comprehensive record. You can't. You just don't know enough. You just can't perceive enough. You're not objective, either. You're alive. You're subjective. You have vested interests—at least in yourself, at least usually.[9]

Peterson highlights the danger of assuming reason communicates the full truth (or even partial truth) about the way things are with the world, including within ourselves. The complexity of existence, both within and external to the self, renders reality opaque at best. This is especially the case, Peterson notes, when things fall apart, when there is a crisis, a breakdown, a tragedy that shatters the tenuous patterns we've constructed to organize life and give it meaning. Best, then, not to be arrogant, best not to presume your way of seeing things is *the* way things should be seen. Best to consult others, to ask

---

7. Peterson, 262.

8. For a helpful overview of the meaning and moral importance of humility, see Christopher Kaczor's article, "Humility: Underrated, Misunderstood, and Still More Important Than Ever," *Angelus,* November 10, 2019, https://angelusnews.com/faith/does-humility-matter-only-if-love-matters/.

9. Peterson, *12 Rules for Life*, 237.

them questions and sincerely listen to their responses. Best, that is, to assume the person you are speaking to might know something you don't.

That's living with humility, which is the only way you can approximate living closer to the truth. Peterson concludes the chapter by counseling, "So, listen, to yourself and those with whom you are speaking. Your wisdom then consists not of the knowledge you already have, but the continual search for knowledge, which is the highest form of wisdom."[10]

Sounding Familiar

As with Peterson's arguments on meaning and courage, his conception of truth-telling, the danger of idolizing human reason, and the consequent necessity for humility has deep resonance in Christianity. St. Augustine, for example, not only wrote an entire treatise against lying—which concludes with the lines "It clearly appears . . . that those testimonies of Scripture have no other meaning than that we must never at all tell a lie"[11]—but one of the primary themes in his *Confessions* is how reason, improperly defined and exercised, can be an obstacle to apprehending the fullness of truth.

For example, just before his conversion in the garden with his friend Alypius, Augustine laments, "What is wrong with us. . . . The unlearned arise and take heaven by force, and here are we with all our learning, stuck fast in flesh and blood!"[12] Having spent his young adulthood intellectually engaging (and, in his mind, defeating) rival philosophies and religions, he comes to the conclusion that the *true* truth, the full truth, truth in and of itself, not only escapes the searching power of his mind; his mind can, in fact, be an obstacle to the truth itself. The only solution, he recognizes, is thus to subordinate his intellect to his will—to *force* himself to recognize his own limits—and, in turn, to subordinate his will to God. Augustine identifies this act of surrender, this act of total humility, as the moment he

---

10. Peterson, 255–256.
11. Augustine, *De mendacio* (*On Lying*) 42.
12. Augustine, *Confessions* (Park Ridge, IL: Word on Fire Classics, 2017), 186.

converts, the moment he finally overcomes his pride: "'How long, how long shall I go on saying tomorrow and again tomorrow? Why not now, why not have an end to my uncleanness this very hour?' Such things I said, weeping in the most bitter sorrow of my heart. And suddenly I heard a voice from some nearby, a boy's voice or a girl's voice, I do not know: but it was a sort of sing-song, repeated again and again, 'Take and read, take and read.'"[13]

Augustine understands the command, emanating from an unseen but real external source: he must open the Bible and read the first passage he sees. He obeys. His finger lands on a verse from St. Paul's Letter to the Romans that ends, "Put on the Lord Jesus Christ, and make no provision for the flesh, to gratify its desires" (Rom. 13:14). The effect is immediate: "In that instant, with the very ending of the sentence, it was as though a light of utter confidence shone in all my heart, and all the darkness of uncertainty vanished away."[14]

By surrendering his intellect in humility (which is not the same as abandoning it), St. Augustine becomes a believer. His conversion is not a rejection of reason. Rather, it is a grounding of reason in that which transcends it, which, he recognizes, is the only way it can properly function. It is the only way he can put his doubts to rest while still allowing his curiosity, his will to understand, to continue searching—not in the sense of looking for something that is unknown or lost but rather in the sense of more deeply comprehending that which he has found (or, better put, that which has found him). Humility thus doesn't obstruct or violate reason for Augustine. It fixes it.

St. Thomas Aquinas is also careful to circumscribe the limits of reason and to locate rationality within the horizon of transcendence. He argues, for example, that reason *can* demonstrate a) that God exists, b) that God created the world, and c) that God exists as the highest good of everything in the world, including human beings. However, he emphasizes that apprehending the fullness of truth, which includes the character of God—the fullness of who God is, what God does, and why God does it—and the *fullness* of God's

---

13. Augustine, 194.
14. Augustine, 195.

creation, falls sharply outside reason's grasp. Aquinas commences the *Summa theologiae*, perhaps the greatest testament to the power of human reason ever written, stating,

> Man is directed to God, as to an end that surpasses the grasp of his reason: "The eye has not seen, O God, besides You, what things You have prepared for them that wait for You" (Isa. 66:4). But the end must first be known by men who are to direct their thoughts and actions to the end. Hence it was necessary for the salvation of man that certain truths which exceed human reason should be made known to him by divine revelation.[15]

In other words, reason can't know everything it needs to know by its own light. Whatever it can tell us about the nature of existence and how to live (and it can tell us a lot) is but a sliver of what actually *is*. We must never, therefore, imagine that the truths that our reason reveals constitute the fullness of Truth itself. We need "outside" help.

Two biblical principles found this epistemic humility in Augustine, Aquinas, and the Christian tradition more broadly: 1) the prohibition of idolatry, and 2) Jesus' command, in the form of Beatitudes (blessings), to be meek and poor in spirit. The prohibition of idolatry given to Moses in the form of the first commandment—"I am the LORD your God . . . you shall have no other gods before me" (Exod. 20:2–3)—is, from a biblical perspective, already embedded in the very act of creation in the words, "In the beginning when God created . . ." (Gen. 1:1). The recognition that God creates the world and everything within it lays down two foundational principles: a) God exists "outside" creation (meaning God is not one being among others in existence), and consequently, b) nothing in creation, nothing in the world, is God. These two principles constitute the foundation upon which every other biblical principle—ontological, epistemic, anthropological, or moral—finds its grounding.

---

15. Thomas Aquinas, *Summa theologiae* 1.1.1.

Applied to the question at hand, these principles mean not only that human beings are not gods (though that doesn't logically rule out God becoming human), but also that human reason in particular is not God. Indeed, while the Bible sees reason as a divinely endowed natural characteristic and therefore fundamentally good, it is littered with instances of both saints and sinners doing precisely the *wrong* thing because of their reason: for example, Adam, Eve, and Cain reasoning they could hide from God; Abraham reasoning he could escape danger by offering his wife sexually to Pharaoh; the liberated Hebrew people reasoning that slavery was preferable to freedom; David's reasoning that killing the pious Uriah could conceal his infidelity with Bathsheba; Judas reasoning that he could sell Jesus out and be content with the profits; even Peter reasoning that denying Jesus three times (which means he had time to think about it) was necessary to save his own life. The Bible sees reason as good, in other words, but also chronicles how it gets us into deep trouble when we decouple it from the will of God—that is, when we rationalize in service of our pride rather than reason.

Responding to the danger of pride is also at the heart of Jesus' formulation of the New Law, which, he emphasizes, is the fulfillment of the Old Testament Law, not its abandonment (see Matt. 5:17). In Matthew's Gospel in particular, the evangelist associates "meekness" and being "lowly of heart" with godliness, even declaring that Christ, himself, is meek: "Take my yoke upon you, and learn from me; for I am gentle and humble in heart, and you will find rest for your souls" (Matt. 11:29).

"Poverty of spirit" and "meekness" are two traits that Friedrich Nietzsche not only found as paradigmatically representative of the Christian religion but manipulatively and odiously so. Nietzsche sees Christianity as a religion of envy, a religion that seduces its adherents into believing that power—which, for Nietzsche, is the only thing that exists in an absolute sense in reality—is evil and that its corollary, weakness, is good. In this inversion, the atheist philosopher argues that Christianity becomes a cult of cowards who conspire to prevent the dominant among the human race from realizing their authentic wills to power. Peterson highlights this feature of Nietzsche's argument in his analysis of resentment. He quotes,

> "Will to equality shall henceforth be the name for virtue; and against all that that has power we want to raise our clamor!" You preachers of equality, the tyrant-mania of impotence clamors thus out of you for equality: your most secret ambitions to be tyrants thus shroud themselves in words of virtue.[16]

"Poverty of spirit" and "meekness" play directly into this narrative of weaponized hypocrisy: Christians are not wolves in sheep's clothing; they are all sheep who wish they could be wolves.

Nietzsche's critique of hypocrisy may be spot on (it's one of the few universal vices), but his description of Christian morality is exactly backward: poorness in spirit is not a coward's ruse to gain worldly power; rather, it is a believer's courage to reject worldly power. This interpretation helps explain Satan's three temptations of Christ at the beginning of Jesus' ministry (see Matt. 4:1–11)—the temptation to live according to material comfort alone (turning rocks into bread), the temptation to misperceive God as a personal genie under one's control ("throw yourself down"), and the temptation to interpret power as dominance over others (making oneself king over all kingdoms)—but there is a commonsensical, practical truth behind the principle of meekness as well: the game of life, played by its own rules and its own rules alone, is ultimately one that everyone loses. There is nothing gained that will not be lost, no triumph that lasts forever, no social or professional perch that will not be occupied by a competitor or come crumbling down altogether. This is so obvious as to render it embarrassing to state, akin to observing, "You know, you *will* die someday." But the heart of human conceit beats eternal in a temporal sense, and each of us believes—or at least acts like we believe—that we are the exception. That is sin, which I'll address more in a

---

16. Quoted in Peterson, *12 Rules for Life*, 288.

subsequent chapter. The point here is that meekness is the antidote to this conceit; it is to live in accordance with the nature of reality rather than in an easily debunked yet nevertheless durable prideful fantasy. Indeed, as Pope Benedict XVI observes, all temptation ultimately emerges from pride:

> At the heart of all temptations . . . is the act of pushing God aside because we perceive him as secondary, if not actually superfluous and annoying, in comparison with all the apparently far more urgent matters that fill our lives. Constructing a world by our own lights, without reference to God, building on our own foundation; refusing to acknowledge the reality of anything beyond the political and the material, while setting God aside as an illusion—that is the temptation that threatens us in many varied forms.[17]

A disposition of humility is thus the only way to overcome this temptation to pride, this temptation to *delusion*; it is, as Benedict puts it, the only way to live with "open" rather than "clutching" hands.[18]

The New Testament also directly connects the humility embedded in meekness to how we perceive our neighbors. Indeed, "love your neighbor" is the biblical version of "assume the person you're listening to might know something you don't." It appears throughout the Bible but is especially palpable in Matthew:

- "Take the log out of your own eye, and then you will see clearly to take the speck out of your neighbor's eye." (Matt. 7:5)

- "But I say to you that if you are angry with a brother or sister, you will be liable to judgment; and if you insult a brother or sister, you will be liable to the council; and if you say, 'You fool,' you will be liable to the hell of fire. So when you are offering your gift at the

---

17. Joseph Ratzinger, *Jesus of Nazareth: From the Baptism in the Jordan to the Transfiguration*, trans. Adrian Walker (New York: Random House, 2007), 28.
18. Ratzinger, 76.

altar, if you remember that your brother or sister has something against you, leave your gift there before the altar and go; first be reconciled to your brother or sister, and then come and offer your gift." (Matt. 5:22–24)

- "You have heard that it was said, 'You shall love your neighbor and hate your enemy.' But I say to you, Love your enemies and pray for those who persecute you, so that you may be children of your Father in heaven; for he makes his sun to rise on the evil and on the good, and sends rain on the righteous and on the unrighteous. For if you love those who love you, what reward do you have? Do not even tax collectors do the same? And if you greet only your brothers and sisters, what more are you doing than others? Do not even the Gentiles do the same? Be perfect, therefore, as your heavenly Father is perfect." (Matt. 5:43–48)

Note that in each of these instances Jesus teaches that "the other"—including one's enemies—has something important to teach us, something we will miss, to our own perdition, if we only focus on ourselves. The other reveals our moral hypocrisy, the insincerity of our worship, the constricted circles of our concern for others, even the illusion that the world is properly meant only for me and not for all human beings, including my enemies. This is not a rejection of the category of evil itself or a rejection of the reality that there are, in fact, evil people in the world. Nor is it a condemnation of making judgments, including judgments about other people. Rather, it is a warning against individual pride and a divine reminder that you (I) might be the problem, might be the guilty one, rather than or in addition to those around you (me).

Finally, the biblical tradition also has its own injunction to specificity in speech. Jesus says in the Gospel of Matthew, "Let your word be 'Yes, Yes' or 'No, No'; anything more than this comes from the evil one" (Matt. 5:37). This is not only a prohibition against using deceptive words; it is also a condemnation of trafficking in ambiguity more generally, a principle that also is vividly on display in the book of Revelation, when the angel of the Lord warns, "I know your works; you are neither cold nor hot. I wish that you were either cold or hot. So, because you are lukewarm, and neither cold nor hot, I am about to spit you out of my mouth" (Rev. 3:15–16). Being mealymouthed is not a mere foible from a biblical standpoint. It is a sign of internal corruption.[19]

False Starts

As these examples illustrate, Peterson's warnings against pride, both in general and epistemically (making human reason and its conclusions the objects of worship) have deep echoes throughout the biblical tradition. But again we can ask: So what? Peterson repeatedly recognizes how deeply Christianity has influenced his philosophy and psychology. Is there really a need to ground his insights in a real doctrine of God? Can't we just use what we need from Christianity and discard the "Christ" part, like extracting a fruit from its husk?

No. As with Peterson's conceptions of meaning and its pursuit, his ideas on truth-telling, reason, and pride ultimately fall apart unless they are grounded in a theological foundation. The reason why this is the case takes the form of an answer to this question: How can I identify truth as truth (including the truth necessary to speak precisely) without idolizing reason? Answering this is not easy because, as Peterson's argument amply demonstrates, we, on the one hand, need to speak the truth and speak it precisely for all the reasons he highlights, while on the other hand, it's also true that reason—the preeminent faculty we use to ascertain truth—can think us into a delusional pride that distorts our vision of reality and leads to individual and social ruin. How, then, can we thread this needle?

---

19. For a helpful overview of the effects of internal integrity on society, see Christopher Kaczor's article, "Is Lying Ever Justified?", *Public Discourse*, September 25, 2015, https://www.thepublicdiscourse.com/2015/09/15606/.

There are two responses that don't rely on a doctrine of God, but neither is adequate. The first is to embrace a form of relativism, claiming, "There is no truth." This may solve the problem of idolizing human reason because relativism denies that reason can know any objective truth. However, the cost is to jettison reason itself, and the cost of *that* is to obliterate Peterson's truth-telling rules: if there is no truth, then it's impossible not to lie because there is no truth (and thus no lies to tell either). Consequently, being precise in one's speech also becomes meaningless because, no matter how specifically you formulate what you say, the *content* of your speech will be arbitrary, disconnected from any objectivity, no different substantively from making tight bursts of nonsensical sound. This holds even when the relativist says, "I may not be able to speak *the* truth, but I can speak *my* truth." If there is no "the" beyond anyone's "my," then we're back to the same problem: arbitrariness and mutual intelligibility. This option literally doesn't make any sense.

The second response is to reply, "I'm not saying there is no truth, just that the *real* truth is *not* what I am saying it is." Put differently, the truth exists, but it is always different from any specific claim about its content. Like relativism, this option effectively addresses the problem of idolizing reason by denying anyone the ability to claim that they are speaking "the truth." Unlike relativism, this model doesn't reject the existence of truth per se, which is a relative strength to its credit. However it, too, ultimately comes at the cost of logical consistency. Saying "I don't believe what I believe to be true is true" is both self-contradictory and impossible to pull off cognitively: How can one think "this is true" (and that's why I'm saying it) and "this is not true" in the same way at the same time?

It is crucial to note that this is different from saying, "I believe this *might* be true." That can be said without inconsistency because claiming something might be true means that it is possible, at least conceptually, to believe it as true, to believe one *is* speaking the truth.[20] The "truth-is-always-elsewhere"

---

20. Peterson has emerged as one of the strongest advocates for freedom of speech, both in the sense of having the freedom *to* speak what one believes to be true *and* the freedom *from* being compelled to say something one does not believe to be true. One of the reasons he identifies why freedom of speech is central to human life is because people must be free to speak in order to be able to pursue the truth. This

option, in contrast, affirms that it is impossible to speak the truth because the truth, whatever it is, is always "over there" in relation to my "here," which means that whenever I move, it moves too. Objectivity exists formally in this model but can have no substantive content, which, in effect, makes it a form of functional relativism. It would thus destroy Peterson's rules as well.

How, then, to proceed? It's not clear how Peterson's argument can respond at this point. He is right to condemn the idolatry of reason and right to call all people to speak truth as precisely as possible. However, he doesn't offer a metaphysical framework that can authorize the use of reason to speak in this way while, at the same time, preventing reason from drifting into epistemic, if not political, totalitarianism. He's got the problem spot on, in other words, but hasn't offered an adequate solution.[21]

The Theological Horizon

Here's a possible way forward: locate both reason and truth on a theistic foundation within a theistic horizon. Place both, in other words, within the mystery of God—which is precisely what the Christian tradition does. First, it is crucial to note that "mystery" in this context does not mean that nothing can be known. It also does not mean *anything* could potentially be true (e.g., square circles, mountains without valleys, 2+2=5). Rather, thinking and speaking in a horizon of mystery means knowing that some things can be known and knowing that some things can't be known. It includes both

---

presumes, of course, that "the truth" is not reducible to subjective utterances of preferences; otherwise there would be nothing to "pursue."

21. One of the difficulties in assessing Peterson's argument in this arena is that he has a pragmatic conception of truth, meaning, broadly, that he conceives of truth only in relation to its utility (in his thought, for example, the utility of reducing suffering). Pragmatic conceptions of truth are different from correspondence theories of truth, which we see, for example, in the Catholic tradition. Unlike pragmatic theories of truth, correspondence theories of truth seek to identify the "truth qua truth" conceptually independent of what relationship it may have to "utility." Examining the relationship between the two theories is deeply complex, but it is important to note that one of the potential problems of pragmatic theories is that they still need to establish some foundation for their definition of "utility" beyond the tautological "utility is that which is useful." In other words, they need a *true* definition of utility to work; and in order to get a true definition, it's not clear how they can avoid embracing some form of the correspondence theory of truth. In this sense, those who are interested in discussing "the truth qua truth" may have more in common with the Catholic tradition than with Jordan Peterson.

the confidence that we really can grow in understanding the truth and the humility that we do not now know the fullness of truth. In other words, the theological horizon of mystery recognizes both the existence of truth and the capacity to apprehend that truth; yet that recognition is always couched within an equally foundational recognition that the apprehension is partial.

This, for example, explains why St. Thomas Aquinas quotes the prophet Isaiah on how God and only God knows that totality of truth while also using reason to offer proofs for God's existence; it explains what St. Augustine means when he calls for surrendering our mind to the will of God after having used reason to explore every other option; it explains why St. Paul affirms the existence of a universal and universally known morality (see Rom. 2:14), while also proclaiming, "We walk by faith, not by sight" (2 Cor. 5:7). Yet perhaps Pope Benedict XVI best captures this insight when he writes,

> The conditions relevant to the knowledge of God are necessarily of a particular kind. In this question, we are not analyzing isolated fragments of reality that we might in some way take into our hands, verify experientially, and then master. This question regards, not that which is below us, but that which is above us. It regards not something we could dominate, but that which exercises its lordship over us and over the whole of reality. . . . This does not mean that we have entered the sphere of the irrational. On the contrary, *what we are looking for is the very foundation of all rationality; we are inquiring into how its light can be perceived.*[22]

For Benedict, and for the Catholic tradition more broadly, reason has the power to seek its own source, and, in doing so, learn both the truth *and* the truth that there is a truth that makes the knowledge of the truth itself possible; or, as Benedict puts it, to learn that there is a reality that makes it possible for the light of reason to see anything at all. That *beyond* and *before* human reason is the horizon of the mystery of God. This horizon is

---

22. Joseph Ratzinger, *Christianity and the Crisis of Cultures*, trans. Brian McNeil (San Francisco: Ignatius Press, 2006), 89–90 (emphasis added).

the inextricable relationship between faith and reason. It is, ultimately, the answer to the question of how we can both speak the truth while recognizing the radical incompleteness of our speech and to do so without falling into relativism or skepticism.

The horizon of mystery is also the foundation of authentic humility. Having grasped both the truth and the limits of my grasp, how could I possibly claim I know all there is? How could I possibly claim that my mind has reined in and tamed the very existence that created both my mind and that which my mind seeks to apprehend? What a pathetic idol reason severed from its transcendent horizon reveals itself to be! How cramped! How distorted!

The horizon changes everything. Who, in his right mind, worships a candle once he realizes its sole purpose is to help guide him toward the dawn? Likewise, who in his right mind thinks that his light and his light alone can guide the path forward? Once I see that what I see is not the totality of the truth, I also see other people, perhaps for the first time. I see them in their alterity—in their otherness—and not merely as empty abstractions or potential resources (or obstacles) for satisfying my desires. If I take God to exist, well, then, they must exist as well; they must have something to do with the same God who created me. They must be I's like me. Perhaps I should listen to them. Perhaps, even, I should love them, maybe, even, as much as I love myself. Maybe, even, if they don't love me.

At the end of the day, placing Peterson's rules within a theistic horizon at once preserves his penetrating insights about truth, truth-telling, reason, and the dangers of idolatry while also explaining how those insights can be true. Indeed, it is only within the horizon of the mystery of God, in the end, that it is possible to know fully anything at all. And if true knowledge is the precondition for true love (how could it be otherwise?), then mystery, too, is ultimately the condition for the possibility of true love.

And true love, in turn, is the only durable antidote to pride.

CHAPTER 9

The Problem of True Love

Ah, true love.

Sadly, gone are the days when these words were sighed (with an overwrought French accent), and a heart still capable of fluttering. Indeed, the statement used to be a question, *the* question. But secularity has long denuded it. Like an overbearing adult flipping on the lights in the middle of the longest slow song, secularity has come to announce, "Sorry, kids, no mystery here: love is just love. Nothing to see and no more to say."

And yet they keep repeating it. "Love is love" appears everywhere nowadays, on bumper stickers (on electric scooters), pegged to university office doors, sewn onto backpacks, nestled in elementary school curricula, and even on public-service ads between Food Network and HGTV lifestyle shows, one featuring former WWE wrestler John Cena informing (warning?) us that "love has no labels."[1] It's so obvious that we need to be reminded of it constantly.

But what does it mean? Asking the question risks revealing your unenlightenment, but perhaps it's a risk worth taking given its importance. How could love have no labels at all? It must have at least one label, right? Otherwise, love could mean anything, anything the individual wants it to mean, only limited by desire. The result would be chaos. All relationships would be reduced to transactional encounters based on perceived mutual self-interest with nothing to sustain them beyond physical, financial, and emotional utility!

---

1. WWE, "'We Are America' with John Cena and Love Has No Labels," YouTube video, July 4, 2016, https://youtu.be/DqZsJrzC9aY.

Oh. I see. Maybe that was the plan all along it. Maybe "love is love" was never intended to be defined because that might spoil the fun. And the only people who spoil fun, the same advocates remind us, are haters.

And no one wants to be a hater.

Down, Monster

But Peterson, prophet of our age on this question, knows better. Love isn't love. Love isn't even like. Indeed, true love isn't at all about what you desire. It's about what you *will*, and the only standard for determining whether your will is right is whether it is willing what is good, whether you want the good or not. This is the conception of love—which Peterson analyzes more broadly in terms of moral regard for oneself and others—that lies at the heart of rules two, three, and five in *12 Rules for Life*. It sets the standard both for how to love others and for how to love yourself.

To understand Peterson's argument, however, we first need to appreciate his anthropology, his conception of human nature. The answer, bluntly, is that we are basically bad, mean, and rotten, not to the core, but pretty close. This corruption applies both to children and to adults for Peterson, since, he argues, bad people must come from somewhere. He recognizes that physical and social factors can have pernicious influences on moral development. Yet he maintains that the primary origins of our individual and collective wickedness are not environmental. People are bad because they choose to be bad, no matter what kind of circumstances they are born into. And the meanness starts early in life. As Peterson observes,

> Scared parents think that a crying child is always sad or hurt. This is simply not true. Anger is one of the most common reasons for crying. Careful analysis of the musculature patterns of crying children has confirmed this . . . . Anger-crying is often an act of dominance and should be dealt with as such.[2]

---

2. Jordan B. Peterson, *12 Rules for Life: An Antidote to Chaos* (New York: Penguin Books, 2019), 128.

There is a raging animal in all of us, for Peterson, even when we're still in onesies. But it's even worse than that. Animals rage because they are hungry and want to stay alive. We, on the other hand, rage even when we are fat and safe, as evidenced by every baby ever. As Peterson writes,

> Dogs are predators. So are cats. . . . They're predators, but it's just their nature. They do not bear responsibility for it. They're hungry, not evil. They don't have the presence of mind, the creativity—and, above all, the self-consciousness—necessary for the inspired cruelty of man.[3]

Peterson occasionally refers to this tendency as "sin," which is a theme I'll address in more depth in chapter 10. But his main point is this: we cannot use desire as the standard for determining what is good, both for children and adults, because we frequently are desiring bad things, which includes the desire to dominate others and cause them harm.[4]

The solution to this problem is a combination of discipline and correct socialization, recognizing that every person needs others not just to keep them in line, to keep them from destroying themselves and society, but also to help them to achieve full flourishing. This starts with establishing the right relationship between parents and children, and adults and children, more broadly. As Peterson writes,

> Because children, like other human beings, are not only good, they cannot simply be left to their own devices, untouched by society, and bloom into perfection. . . . [The necessity for socialization] means that it is not just

---

3. Peterson, 54.
4. This claim may seem to fly in the face of conventional wisdom: Isn't what people desire, by definition, good for them? How could they desire it if it weren't? I will address below how it is possible to understand desire and goodness as consonant. However, Peterson's point here is that there is something *distinctive* about human nature that results in our desires and our good sometimes (if not frequently) being at odds with each other. This is also a rejection of the view of humanity put forth, most famously by Jean Jacques Rousseau, that children come into the world as morally perfect—"noble savages" in Rousseau's language—but then are only later corrupted by society. Peterson sees the reverse as true, at least to some degree, and, in doing so, is embracing something akin to the Christian conception of original sin.

wrong to attribute all violent tendencies of human beings to the patholo-gies of social structure. It's wrong enough to be virtually backward. The vital process of socialization prevents much harm and fosters much good. Children must be shaped and informed, or they cannot thrive.[5]

If you love your children, in other words, you don't let them do things that prevent them from growing up into well-functioning adults who contribute to the good of society. That is not only good for society. That is what is good for them. Whether they realize that or want to do it is beside the point. This approach to child-rearing is commonsensical for Peterson, yet he observes how frequently it comes as news to contemporary parents.

Indeed, Peterson trenchantly illustrates his commitment to this princi-ple—even with other people's children—recalling a story of how he, while babysitting another couple's two-year-old, was able to get the obstreperous child to sleep. The boy's father tells Peterson that the only way the boy will go to bed is if he gets to watch Elmo. Peterson recalls thinking, "There's no damn way I'm rewarding a recalcitrant child for unacceptable behaviour . . . and I'm certainly not showing anyone any Elmo video."[6] The battle with the boy ensues, and a persistent Peterson, willing to exercise his authority, eventually wins:

I glanced back, to check his position, one last time. He was back on his feet. I pointed my finger at him. "Down, monster," I said and I meant it. He went down like a shot. I closed the door. We liked each other. Neither my wife nor I heard a peep out of him for the rest of the night.[7]

To love a child is not to reward the inner monster, nor to pacify it. It is to teach her or him that monsters will not be tolerated and, in doing so, to give their inner potential for becoming a good person a fighting chance.

5. Peterson, *12 Rules for Life*, 122.
6. Peterson, 128.
7. Peterson, 129.

Auto-nomos?

"But," comes the likely reply, "that's just for kids. Maybe we can discipline kids for their own good, but certainly that doesn't apply to adults. We are, after all, autonomous. That's what it means to be a grown up: we get to do what we want."

To quote Inigo Montoya, "You keep using that word; I do not think it means what you think it means." "Autonomy" comes from the Greek words for "law" (*nomos*) and "self" (*auto*). To be autonomous is to be a law to oneself, which means that autonomy is about imposing *limits* and sticking to those limits—recognizing the limits as *law*—not doing what one pleases.[8]

Yet the deeper problem, even if we assume autonomy means doing what one pleases within fixed limits, is that, as Peterson observes, we, as a species, have a hard time discerning what *should* please us.[9] Evolutionary biologists may point to the basics: Everyone wants to stay alive and avoid preventable pain, right? Of course! But also, maybe not. Peterson begins his chapter on rule two, "Treat yourself like someone you are responsible for helping," for example, by observing the shocking prevalence of people who fail to take life-saving medicine, even when they can afford it, including in cases of otherwise successful kidney transplants.[10]

But those must be crazy people, you might think. *I take my medicine. I never knowingly do anything to harm myself.* Yes, only crazy people do that.

8. For example, contrary to many contemporary proponents of autonomy, Kant—the philosophical father of the modern conception of autonomy—understood the principle as categorically prohibiting a person from committing suicide based on the principle that you must treat all human beings as ends in themselves, including yourself. In his *Groundwork for the Metaphysics of Morals*, he wrote, "He who contemplates suicide should ask himself whether his action can be consistent with the idea of humanity as an end in itself. If he destroys himself in order to escape from painful circumstances, he uses a person merely as a mean to maintain a tolerable condition up to the end of life. But a man is not a thing, that is to say, something which can be used merely as means, but must in all his actions be always considered as an end in himself. I cannot, therefore, dispose in any way of a man in my own person so as to mutilate him, to damage or kill him." In other words, autonomy does *not* mean doing whatever you may want, even with your own life.

9. Another way of putting this point is that all of us have multiple and sometimes conflicting desires. The question then becomes *which* desires should be satisfied. Since desires are not static, we can grow to desire things and our desires for other things fade away. Since our desires can be cultivated, we face the question "Which desires should I cultivate?"

10. Peterson, *12 Rules for Life*, 32–33.

Normal people take their medications. But normal people also eat too much, drink too much, work too much (or not enough), don't spend enough time at the gym (or too much), form toxic relationships (or don't have relationships at all), cheat on their spouses, engage in dangerous sexual behavior, take pleasure in negativity, and do nothing as they watch their lives fall apart from preventable causes. This, for Peterson, sums up the folly of using desire as a standard for identifying what you and others should be doing. Doing what you want and only what you want is poison. As he writes,

> To treat yourselves as if you were someone you are responsible for helping . . . is to consider what is truly good for you. This is not "what you want." It is also not "what would make you happy." . . . "Happy" is by no means synonymous with "good." You must get children to brush their teeth. They must put on their snowsuits when they go outside in the cold, even though they might object strenuously. You must help a child become a virtuous, responsible, awake being, capable of full reciprocity—able to take care of himself and others, and to thrive while doing do. Why would you think it acceptable to do anything less for yourself?[11]

Loving yourself, in short, is not about self-indulgence. Loving yourself is not doing whatever you want. It's the opposite. It's doing what is good even though you don't want to.

This principle also transfers to how we should love other people. Loving others means calling them to the highest standards of the good. As he writes,

> Every good example [of character] is a fateful challenge, and every hero, a judge. Michelangelo's great perfect marble David cries out to its observer: "You could be more than you are." When you dare aspire upward, you reveal the inadequacy of the present and the promise of the future. Then you disturb others, in the depths of their souls, where they understand that their cynicism and immobility are unjustifiable. You play Abel to

---

11. Peterson, 62.

their Cain. You remind them that they ceased caring not because of life's horrors, which are undeniable, but because they do not want to lift the world up on their shoulders, where it belongs.[12]

Don't feel good, Peterson exhorts. *Be good.* If you really love others—child, spouse, friend, coworker, even acquaintance—don't, to the extent it is possible and appropriate, let them be anything else than the best possible expression of what it means to be human. Hold yourself to the same standard and surround yourself with others who will guide you, push you if necessary, back on the path of the good when your desires lure you off.

You Have Heard It Said

As with the previous rules, Peterson's description of moral regard for oneself and others—what I am describing as Peterson's conception of love—has deep biblical resonance. Yet while the overlap is evident, contemporary portrayals of Christianity may give the impression that Peterson's account of love is, in fact, foreign to "Christian values." In the eyes of many, both secular and believer, two words sum up what it means to be Christian: don't judge. Any form of negative moral evaluation (advocates of this view don't take issue with positive judgments) is not only prohibited but evidence of one's moral corruption. They claim there is biblical support for this view in Jesus' words, "Do not judge, so that you may not be judged." Passing negative judgment is thus seen as hypocritical at best and dispositive evidence that you're a bad person at worst.

What, though, does the relevant passage actually say? Here it is in its entirety:

> "Do not judge, so that you may not be judged. For with the judgment you make you will be judged, and the measure you give will be the measure you get. Why do you see the speck in your neighbor's eye, but do not notice the log

---

12. Peterson, 89.

in your own eye? Or how can you say to your neighbor, 'Let me take the speck out of your eye,' while the log is in your own eye? You hypocrite, first take the log out of your own eye, and then you will see clearly to take the speck out of your neighbor's eye." (Matt. 7:1–5)

Jesus is not judging judging here.[13] He is condemning hypocrisy, holding others to a standard that you do not abide by yourself. That is something entirely different. Indeed, the same passage implicitly authorizes the judgment of others—"*then* you will see clearly" (emphasis added)—provided the person making the judgment is in a state of moral rectitude.

In fact, making judgments about the rightness or wrongness of actions (which is different than judging intentions) is such a fundamental part of biblical morality that it is impossible to interpret the meaning of key passages without presuming both a) humans have the capacity to distinguish between good and evil, and b) what it means to be a follower of Jesus is not only to make the personal choice for good but to counsel others to do the same. Think, for example, of Jesus' words, also in the Gospel of Matthew, "Be perfect, therefore, as your heavenly Father is perfect" (Matt. 5:48), or when he cautions that "the gate is wide and the road is easy that leads to destruction, and there are many who take it" (Matt. 7:13). How could we possibly interpret what Jesus means here without presuming that we are making judgments? And lest we think that he is only calling individuals to judge themselves, Jesus makes it clear that his followers are *obligated* to judge the acts of others, as well:

---

13. It is important to note that the Catholic moral tradition has long distinguished between a) the objective morality of an action itself, and b) the subjective guilt an individual may or may not have in performing the action. In the event of a suicide, for example, we can recognize suicide as objectively and categorically wrong (meaning it should never be done), while also recognizing that some who have committed suicide have done so under circumstances of extreme psychological trauma, which raises serious questions about whether or not they can be held responsible for their action. Applied to "judging" more broadly, the basic biblical insight is that we are, indeed, called to judge immoral actions; however, that does not mean we are necessarily authorized to judge the *subjective* guilt of the person committing the immoral acts. Only God, Christians believe, knows the true subjective guilt (or lack of guilt) of an individual. That doesn't mean human beings are not responsible for their sin; it only means that we must exercise extreme caution in making pronouncements, judgments, that someone is "a bad person."

"If another member of the church sins against you, go and point out the fault when the two of you are alone. If the member listens to you, you have regained that one. But if you are not listened to, take one or two others along with you, so that every word may be confirmed by the evidence of two or three witnesses. If the member refuses to listen to them, tell it to the church; and if the offender refuses to listen even to the church, let such a one be to you as a Gentile and a tax collector." (Matt. 18:15–17)

Another paradigmatic example of the necessity of making judgements appears slightly earlier in Matthew when Jesus says,

"If any of you put a stumbling block before one of these little ones who believe in me, it would be better for you if a great millstone were fastened around your neck and you were drowned in the depth of the sea. Woe to the world because of stumbling blocks! Occasions for stumbling are bound to come, but woe to the one by whom the stumbling block comes! If your hand or your foot causes you to stumble, cut it off and throw it away; it is better for you to enter life maimed or lame than to have two hands or two feet and to be thrown into the eternal fire. And if your eye causes you to stumble, tear it out and throw it away; it is better for you to enter life with one eye than to have two eyes and to be thrown into the hell of fire." (Matt. 18:6–9)

This is not the nonjudgmental Jesus of self-esteem culture fantasy. Jesus leaves no doubt for his hearers that it is not only enough to avoid sin yourself; you better be sure that you don't lead others to sin as well, especially the "little ones," who, in context, not only means children but all faithful (i.e., trusting) disciples of Christ. Avoiding sin in this way requires making judgments, very careful judgments, about yourself and about others. And the stakes couldn't be higher: we need to be so committed not to sin and not to lead others to sin that we are willing to cast off a dear part of ourselves (even a "limb" or an "eye") if we suspect it may be leading us or others astray.

I don't mean to suggest that it is easy and obvious to determine what constitutes right judgment based on these passages alone. There are also the fundamental themes of grace and forgiveness, which contextualize everything that Jesus says about moral perfection. I will address those themes in the subsequent chapter. However, what these passages and others like them throughout the New Testament *do* make clear is that human beings are morally obligated to make judgments about themselves and others.

So let's start, therefore, from the premise that making moral judgments is good from a biblical perspective. How, then, do we determine the criteria for what constitutes a good moral judgment and, more broadly, the right way of living, both in relation to others and to oneself? The answer is love. In a question designed to entrap Jesus into misspeaking by choosing the "wrong law," a Pharisee asks Jesus which commandment is the greatest. He replies,

> "'You shall love the Lord your God with all your heart, and with all your soul, and with all your mind.' This is the greatest and first commandment. And a second is like it: 'You shall love your neighbor as yourself.' On these two commandments hang all the law and the prophets." (Matt. 22:37–40)

From the lips of God incarnate comes the answer: *all you need is love.* Love of God and love of neighbor (which mirrors love of self) is the genus within which every other moral requirement is a species. It is the sum total of how we are to live individually and communally.

But *how* do you love in this way? As with the previous questions, St. Augustine and St. Thomas Aquinas offer great insight. In St. Augustine's treatise *The Morals of the Catholic Church,* for example, Augustine argues that every form of morality can ultimately be categorized as a form of virtue (*being* a certain way, and not only acting a certain way), and all virtue, in turn, can be categorized as emerging from the two great commandments: love of God and love of neighbor. Indeed, to love one's neighbor is to do everything possible to assist her or him to love God, who is the highest good of all. He writes,

123

Now, you love yourself suitably when you love God better than yourself. What, then, you aim at in yourself you must aim at in your neighbor— namely, that he may love God with a perfect affection. For you do not love him as yourself, unless you try to draw him to that good which you are yourself pursuing. For this is the one good which has room for all to pursue it along with you. From this precept proceed the duties of human society. . . . But the first thing to aim at is that we should be benevolent— that is, that we cherish no malice and no evil design against another. For man is the nearest neighbor of man.[14]

In this passage, Augustine unites the love of self, the love of neighbor, the love of God, and the Golden Rule (do to others what you would have them do to you). We also see the first rule of justice: do no harm. Augustine emphasizes, however, that merely refraining from interfering negatively in another person's life is not sufficient. It is a sin to inflict harm on another; it is equally sinful not to help when you can. As he writes, "But as a man may sin against another in two ways, either by injuring him or by not helping him when it is in his power, and as it for these things which no loving man would do that men are called wicked, all that is required is, I think, proved by these words, 'The love of our neighbor works no ill.'"[15] This help, moreover, must always be construed as help both to soul *and* body:

Man, then, as viewed by his fellow-man, is a rational soul with a mortal and earthly body in its service. Therefore he who loves his neighbor does good partly to the man's body, and partly to his soul. What benefits the body is called medicine; what benefits the soul, discipline. Medicine here includes everything that either preserves or restores bodily health. It includes, therefore, not only what belongs to the art of medical men, properly so called, but also food and drink, clothing and shelter, and every

---

14. Augustine, *Of the Morals of the Catholic Church* 49.
15. Augustine, 50.

means of covering and protection to guard our bodies against injuries and mishaps from without as well as from within.[16]

Augustine's account of love cannot thus be tagged as a vacuous piety only concerned with "getting to heaven." The good of the body and the good of the soul must never be separated in loving the neighbor. It is also important to emphasize that it is precisely the unity of the love of God and the love of neighbor that gives the latter its objective content. To love the neighbor is not to do what the neighbor wants; it is to do what is good for him, and what is good for him is to help him pursue what is objectively good—namely, a relationship with the good itself, God. This also applies both to how to love oneself (loving yourself is not doing what you want; it is doing what is good for you), and how, turning the tables, the neighbor is to love *you*: just as we are called to offer fraternal correction, we are called to accept it as well.

St. Thomas Aquinas makes a similar argument in the *Summa*. His treatment of love is expansive and profoundly nuanced, but we can capture the heart of it in his discussions of love in the form of friendship and charity, which he considers to be the highest forms of love. Aquinas writes,

> As the Philosopher [Aristotle] says, "to love is to wish good to someone." Hence the movement of love has a twofold tendency: towards the good which a man wishes to someone (to himself or to another) and towards that to which he wishes some good. Accordingly, man has love of concupiscence towards the good that he wishes to another, and love of friendship towards him to whom he wishes good.[17]

To love is to wish good to someone—that is the foundation. Aquinas divides that love, however, into two "movements": one is the object herself or himself of love (which includes the object of love being oneself as well); the second is love as it pertains to the *ultimate* object of love *for* the beloved.

---

16. Augustine, 52.
17. Thomas Aquinas, *Summa theologiae* 1-2.26.4.

An example can help illustrate. In saying I love my wife as a friend (setting aside physical desire, which requires an additional level of analysis), I both love her, meaning she is the object of my affection, and, if my love is authentic, I love what is good for her; indeed, that is what Aquinas means by "concupiscence" in this context: loving my wife means I desire what is truly good for her. In other words, to love my wife is both to love her and what is good for her in such a way that I cannot separate the two without undermining the nature of love itself.

For Aquinas, this definition of love also holds both for strangers (strangers are only "neighbors" you do not have personal acquaintance with, and as such deserve the same moral regard as all individuals) and even for enemies. Aquinas writes, for example,

> Love of one's enemies may be understood in three ways. First, as though we were to love our enemies as such: this is perverse, and contrary to charity, since it implies love of that which is evil in another.
>
> Secondly love of one's enemies may mean that we love them as to their nature, but in general: and in this sense charity requires that we should love our enemies, namely, that in loving God and our neighbor, we should not exclude our enemies from the love given to our neighbor in general.
>
> Thirdly, love of one's enemies may be considered as specially directed to them, namely, that we should have a special movement of love towards our enemies. Charity does not require this absolutely, because it does not require that we should have a special movement of love to every individual man, since this would be impossible.[18]

In the second example here, Aquinas clarifies that to love one's enemy, specifically as it regards their humanity, is the same as to love anyone else: *you will what is good for them.* That does not mean loving those characteristics in them that make them your enemy; that would be "perverse." We should not

---

18. Thomas Aquinas, 2-2.25.8.

love someone's viciousness, just as we should not love the cancer in the sick person. It also does not mean that we must be well-disposed or have good feelings for our enemies; that is what Aquinas means, in the third example, of charity not requiring a "special movement" of love. But it does mean wanting and, to the extent that it is possible, seeking what is good for them, not as enemies but as fellow human beings.

Unsurprisingly, this principle also applies to self-love. Distinguishing between inauthentic (what we might call egoism or selfishness) and authentic self-love, Aquinas writes,

> Those who love themselves are to be blamed, in so far as they love themselves as regards their sensitive nature, which they humor. This is not to love oneself truly according to one's rational nature, so as to desire for oneself the good things which pertain to the perfection of reason: and in this way chiefly it is through charity that a man loves himself.[19]

What "pertains to the perfection of reason" is another way of saying what is objectively good, what is good, *in fact*, and not merely what the individual may perceive as good and desire as such.

Yet, what is objectively good according to reason? Like Augustine, and as is already evident from the passages above, the ultimate good of all human beings is God, and, more specifically, being in right relationship with God. God constitutes every human being's highest good, no matter what they may proximately desire, because God is the good itself; everything else in existence is only truly good insofar as it participates in God's goodness. To love someone, including yourself—including someone who hates you—is thus to help them (me) live in a way that enables, rather than obstructs, the progression toward right relationship with goodness itself. This, as we also see in Augustine, does not mean neglecting the temporal goods of the body. Rather, true love means loving both body and soul and assisting the unity

---

19. Thomas Aquinas, 2-2.25.4.

of both to realize their full humanity as God created it. It is immoral, for Aquinas and the Christian tradition more broadly, to love in any other way.

The Second Is Like Unto the First

Although Peterson does not explicitly make this connection in his rules concerning moral regard, if loving someone means pursuing her or his good, and what is good is to pursue what is meaningful rather than expedient, and what it means to pursue meaning is to "advance Being," then loving necessarily entails assisting others, including oneself, to advance Being. If one's desires are in line with this goal, good. If they are not, as Peterson might say, too bloody bad. You seek what is good for yourself and others whether it aligns with your perceived self-interest or not.

This is remarkably similar to the biblical conception of love. However, we can once again ask the foundational question. Can Peterson's argument stand on its own or does it need a more robust theological foundation to support it?

It does need that foundation, for three reasons. First, as laid out in the chapter on pursuing meaning, "Being" by itself lacks sufficient substance for serving as an ontologically stable and epistemically clear final goal. Insofar as "Being" represents "the good" in this context, it suffers from the same problem. If love means pursuing the good and the good means advancing Being, then once again we need to have greater clarity on what "Being" substantively means. The Christian conception of God, especially complemented with the incarnate Christ, fills that gap.

Second and related, severing the command to love of God from the command to love the neighbor leaves the meaning of "love thy neighbor" so malleable as to render it relative to the individual's own private interpretation. This is, as noted above, because we need a stable definition of God and the goodness of God. Yet it's also because we need a stable definition of "love." Christianity provides this stability. The basic Christian insight that God exists in Trinitarian relation—Father, Son, and Holy Spirit—establishes the standard to which human beings ought to conform in their own acts of love. Drawing on basic Trinitarian theology, the Father, Son, and Holy Spirit can be conceived as the perfect "I," "You," and "We" of God's interior life: God is he who loves, he who is loved, and the relationship between the lover and the beloved. God is one and, as such, is in perfect relationship with himself. There is nothing lacking in this relation, no competition, no dominance of one over the other—just perfect living concordance.

This establishes the foundation for the Christian meaning of love in the first commandment, which, in turn, already points to the second commandment: we are made to love God *as God loves*, which is to be in perfect relation with *whom* God loves—namely, every human being. This also explains why Jesus commands us to love one's neighbor *as oneself*. This is not a license to use one's egotistical self-regard as a model for how to treat others. Rather, it, too, is grounded in Trinitarian love: if I love myself as God loves himself (and as God loves me), then I am internally whole, and, like God, that internal wholeness, that internal integrity of life, leads to a superabundance of life that pours forth out into world and into other people. Loving yourself in the right way, in other words, leads to uncontainable generosity of being.

We get a glimpse of this in the rare moments when we experience joy: we cannot keep it to ourselves. Our internal happiness surges into the world and gives life and buoyancy (or at least tries to) to those around us. (Loving yourself the wrong way, in contrast, reverses the flow, seeking to pull the outside world into oneself for dominance and consumption). This, in sum, helps explain why Jesus so closely links the two great commandments, saying the second is "like" the first: the first provides the model for what the second should be, and living out the second is the concrete application of the first. This is also why we read in 1 John in the New Testament, "Those who say, 'I love God,' but hate their brothers and sisters, are liars; for those who do not love a brother or sister whom they have seen, cannot love God whom they have not seen" (1 John 4:20).

This only scratches the surface of Trinitarian theology, but it gives a sense of how Christianity grounds its conception of love. There is no love of God without love of neighbor, and crucially for the comparison here, there is no love of neighbor without love of God in the sense that there is no objective model for defining the nature of objective love. It is not clear how Peterson's account of love can offer this kind of richness and objective stability in describing both what love is and how we are to love. Consequently, "seeking what is good" risks slipping right back into the relativism Peterson otherwise so firmly rejects.

Third, even if we were to accept that Peterson's account can stand on its own, it offers a bleak view of human life. The reason is because he cuts a sharp line between desire and goodness, so sharp that it appears that what we want and what is good for us are diametrically opposed. This is the problem of puritanism, which takes a similar form in the duty ethics that define the Kantian philosophical tradition, captured in Immanuel Kant's famous dictum, "Happiness is the death of morality." There is great wisdom in this view; it is certainly true that we should always do what is good rather than what we want if the two conflict. But there is great misery as well. Put bluntly, *Who wants to live a life in which you always must act contrary to your desires?* Peterson frequently states in *12 Rules* that life is fundamentally defined by suffering (a theme I'll address in more depth in chapter 10). In this regard, his conception of moral regard leaves the impression that loving authentically not only includes suffering—it undoubtedly does—but *is* suffering.

Yet it doesn't have to be that way. The Christian tradition, especially in its Augustinian roots, shares Peterson's view that human beings are deeply corrupted by perverse self-interest (St. Augustine even has his own reflections on the problem of infants seeking to dominate their parents!) and that this self-interest profoundly twists our desires and our conception of love. Christianity also shares the conclusion that it is categorically wrong to act on desires that are contrary to the good, either in caring for another or for oneself. However, unlike Peterson, Christianity does not sever happiness and morality, or put more simply, being good and being happy. It is sin that tears those two apart, not the nature of human desire or happiness itself. What Christianity offers, therefore, is a path out of sin and, consequently, into the reunification of desire and goodness. It is the path of virtue, the path of sanctification, the path of becoming the kind of people who do the right thing, love in the right way, not because it is our duty to do so (though it is), but rather because it makes us happy to do it; indeed, because we find pleasure, even delight, in doing it. This insight is embedded in the Christian conception of joy, what the great Catholic writer G.K. Chesterton called the "gigantic secret" of Christians.[20] Joyfulness is "gigantic" because having joy, being joyful, lies at the heart of the Christian life. Yet joyfulness remains "secret" not because it is seeking to conceal itself—the opposite is the case: it wants to be seen—but because our brokenness, our sin, constantly pulls us back, individually and socially, into believing, like the dignified but melancholic Eeyore, that a life of following the rules in an otherwise bleak landscape is as good as it gets.

Christianity rejects this conclusion. It not only gets better—it *is* better, even now, even in the thick of the night. Yes, doing the right thing is good, so good that we should always do it. Helping others to do the right thing is good too. But love, true love, promises so much more than the net reduction of suffering as the reward. Peterson is absolutely right to point out that there is a cross on the path of love and that cross will hurt—hurt bad, hurt to the point of death—if you choose to follow it as you should. There's no escaping that. But then that same cross brings you back to life more alive than you could have ever imagined. And there, on the flipside of duty, on the flipside of doing what you were supposed to do, you slowly discover that that doing what you were supposed to do was actually what you most wanted to do— what would make you the most happy—in the first place. It is for this reason St. Augustine can confidently sum up the Christian tradition by declaring, "Love, and do as you will."[21]

Being good will still require work, of course. But laboring in the vineyard of the Lord is always sweet, even when it hurts: "Come to me, all you that are weary and are carrying heavy burdens, and I will give you rest. Take my

---

20. G.K. Chesterton, *Orthodoxy* (Park Ridge, IL: Word on Fire Classics, 2017), 163.
21. Augustine, *Homilies on First John* 7.8.

yoke upon you, and learn from me; for I am gentle and humble in heart, and you will find rest for your souls. For my yoke is easy, and my burden is light" (Matt. 11:28–30).

CHAPTER 10

The Problem of Creation and Redemption

One of the contradictions of contemporary secularism is its worship of nature, on the one hand, and its call for radical liberation from nature, on the other. We are told to eat organically, limit our carbon footprint, protect wild spaces, take public transportation, ditch our lawns, move into high-rise apartments (the least impactful form of housing, they say), and stop having resource-consuming children. We are also told we can choose if we are a male or a female (or something else entirely), that there are no natural differences between the sexes, that we can have intercourse without thinking about reproduction, that babies in wombs are not human life (unless they become "chosen"), that it is "ableist" to distinguish—physically, not morally—between abled and disabled human bodies, and, thanks to the transhumanist movement, that the future of humanity lies in integrating computer circuity into our brains. Nature, in short, now finds itself playing the role of a pitiable idol in an abusive relationship: it's bowed down to in cultish reverence one moment, then whipped, cursed, spit on, lashed to a metallic table, and tortured the next—only to be worshiped again in contrived wails of repentance.

Of Lobsters and Men

Peterson recognizes that this bipolarity is not natural. His approach is more balanced. It doesn't worship nature. Nor does it dismiss nature as morally neutral fodder for indiscriminate manipulation. Indeed, his understanding is deeply complex. It is thus helpful to divide his thought into categories that Peterson doesn't explicitly use but nevertheless are evident in his work.

The first is "nature" with a little "n." This is nature in the form of the patterns evident in the natural world, patterns that are associated with evolutionary development and the regulation of life. Peterson's argument in this category is twofold: 1) Human nature is rooted in nature itself, which means humanity evinces behaviors evident in other species; and 2) human nature is unique, meaning that our relationship with nature qua nature is open to interpretation.

The first pillar of Peterson's argument on little "n" nature is evident in his now famous analysis of lobsters. Lobsters, he observes, naturally organize themselves into "dominance hierarchies." These hierarchies are pyramidal structures of power, which emerge as the most "successful" lobsters—those most effective at securing sustenance, defending territory, and attracting mates—rise to the top; those who are relatively less successful occupy lower levels, descending downward to the "loser" lobsters at the base of the pyramid who can barely survive (and usually don't for long). Peterson's point in his examination of lobsters is that humans and lobsters, from an evolutionary perspective, share deep biochemical similarities that include, among other characteristics, a mechanism for regulating serotonin levels as they pertain to the individual's (lobster or human) perception of his or her place in a dominance hierarchy. As Peterson writes,

> We (the sovereign *we,* the *we* that has been around since the beginning of life) have lived in dominance hierarchies for a long, long time. We were struggling for position before we had skin, or hands, or lungs, or bones.[1]

Hierarchies and the awareness of hierarchies are thus inscribed into our nature. They are literally in our blood and, as such, cannot be extricated from human nature or "nature" more broadly.

1. Jordan Peterson, *12 Rules for Life: An Antidote to Chaos* (New York: Penguin Books, 2019), 14.

Peterson is not celebrating these hierarchies. Many critics who have (willfully) not listened to him carefully accuse him of advocating for social Darwinism. That is nonsense. The only "political" conclusion that one could derive from his empirical observation—and Peterson wants us to draw this conclusion because he thinks it is true—is that social hierarchies are natural, permanently so. It is thus simply not the case that "power structures" qua "power structures" are socially constructed in the sense that they are unnatural or adventitious.[2] If you try to quash one hierarchy, know that another will immediately fills its place, an observation captured in the dictum "Power abhors a vacuum."

The solution for Peterson is thus not to topple all hierarchies, but rather 1) to do everything possible as an individual to resist bullies who seek to prevent you from rising in social hierarchies (i.e., "stand up straight with your shoulders back"), and 2) to work, individually and socially, to multiply the number of hierarchies (what Peterson also refers to as games of competencies) so that as many people as possible can excel at doing what they have an aptitude for, which ultimately benefits everyone.

Peterson's respect for little "n" nature is also evident in his insistence that, ontologically, girls are girls and boys are boys. The reaffirmation of this biological fact is one of the major themes in rule eleven, "Do not bother children when they are skateboarding." Peterson writes,

> Boys' interests tilt towards things; girls' interests tilt towards people. Strikingly, these differences, strongly influenced by biological factors, are most pronounced in the Scandinavian societies where gender-equality has been pushed hardest: this is the opposite of what would be expected by those who insist, ever more loudly, that gender is a social construct. It isn't. This isn't a debate. The data are in.[3]

---

2. Peterson draws on the same observation to reject the thesis that "capitalism" created social hierarchies. He does not dispute that there are, indeed, some unjust hierarchies in capitalist economies. However, he rejects that hierarchies qua hierarchies are a consequence of capitalism itself. They are, rather, rooted in our nature.

3. Peterson, *12 Rules for Life*, 298.

For Peterson, this indisputable empirical fact—a "fact" because it is rooted in nature—points to a commonsensical principle, at least for those not blinded by gender ideologies: let girls be girls and boys be boys, meaning *free* them *to choose* to live according to the natural patterns of their biology. That is the significance of the data from Scandinavian societies: women and men *naturally* choose different occupations and, more broadly, different patterns for structuring their lives when permitted to do so. Forcing women and men into ideologically contrived patterns either directly (having enforceable quotas) or indirectly (shaming companies with perceived gender imbalances as "sexist" based only on numerical gender imbalance) is thus to distort natural human inclinations. It is, to use a meme of our age, "anti-science."

This fixedness of natural variation between women and men also has moral implications. To act against nature is to act against the way things are, and to act against the way things are is to prevent beings from realizing their full, innate potential. It is to render something *less* than it could be and, therefore, less than it is. Applied to human beings, acting against nature prevents individuals from full flourishing, flourishing that is only possible when, like a healthy organ, the individual is allowed to function as he or she was intended to by nature. As Peterson writes,

> I have a nature, and so do you, and so do we all. We must discover that nature, and contend with it, before making peace with ourselves.[4]

Ignoring nature or, worse, seeking to alter it, is analogous to a fish jumping onto dry land and flopping in celebratory defiance of having escaped its aquatic oppression.

It is important to stress, however, that Peterson uses the word "discover" to describe nature. Discovering means more than seeing. It means *looking for*, implying we have more to learn about something that is already there. This, for Peterson, describes the right balance. Our nature is, indeed, objective, but that doesn't mean that our relationship with it is simple to comprehend.

---

4. Peterson, 193.

That goes for the natural world as well. It, too, objectively exists. But that doesn't mean it's immediately clear what disposition we should take to it. We thus have to *interpret* nature, simultaneously seeing it as a fixed part of reality—reality itself—yet also somehow, in limited but real ways, under the influence of our interpretations of it.

This insight defines the second pillar of Peterson's conception of little "n" nature. Humans have a nature, no doubt, but human nature is different from any other kind of nature and even "nature" itself (the sum total of all that exists in the natural world). Being human thus, in Peterson's words, requires a *dance* with nature. He writes,

> The theory of natural selection does not posit creatures matching themselves ever more precisely to a template specified by the world. It is more that creatures are in a dance with nature, albeit a deadly one.[5]

Dancing with nature means that nature, little "n" nature, is fixed in some fundamental sense, the partner we cannot abandon without abandoning our very selves. Yet it is also malleable, governable even. It is dangerous but can be tamed in some ways; we can learn its steps and adapt and even get it to move to our own music. At the same time, we also must recognize that nature can and will surprise, breaking away from our grasp and turning on us. (I write this in month three of the COVID-19 pandemic.) The human dance with nature thus sees nature both as a threat and as an opportunity, as a source of beauty and a source of misery. Sometimes we lead; sometimes it leads. Either way, we must constantly be changing our footing.

Chaos and Order

This feature of little "n" nature points to a deeper understanding of nature in Peterson's thought, what we could call "Nature" with a big "N." This is

---

5. Peterson, 13.

Peterson's metaphysics, his account of what fundamentally *is*. Two forces describe this meta-pattern, each distinct yet inextricably tied to its obverse: chaos and order. As Peterson writes, "[Nature is] chaos, within order, within chaos, within higher order."[6] He further delineates the relationship between the two by drawing on the mythical representations of order as "male" and "chaos" as female, which he also sees represented in the Taoist two serpents symbol:

> Order and chaos are the yang and yin of the famous Taoist symbol: two serpents, head to tail. Order is the white, masculine serpent; Chaos, it's black, feminine counterpart. The black dot in the white—and the white in the black—indicate the possibility of transformation: just when everything seems secure, the unknown can loom, unexpectedly and large. Conversely, just when everything seems lost, new order can emerge from catastrophe and chaos. . . . For the Taoists, meaning is to be found on the border between the ever-entwined pair. To walk that border is to stay on the path of the divine Way.[7]

It is crucial to note that Peterson is not associating "order" with the "good" and "chaos" with the "bad" and, by extension, "male" with the "good" and "female" with the "bad." This has been another point that uncharitable critics of Peterson have used to play gotcha rather than seriously engage his thought. As I will explain below, Peterson's appeal to this duality is not an area of his thinking that I find persuasive, but he has been clear both in *12 Rules* and numerous interviews that "chaos" and "order" are morally neutral and only become a problem when they are out of balance—a point emphasized by the title of the book's sequel: *Beyond Order: 12 More Rules for Life*. In that sense, the "morality" of each principle is a wash: either can be good or bad depending on its relative prevalence in relation to the other.[8]

---

6. Peterson, 13.

7. Peterson, xxviii.

8. For Peterson, pure chaos is completely unsustainable; no individual or community can survive without some order. However, he also sees pure order as totalitarian, which destroys individuals and communities. Hence, the need for balance between the two in his view.

That does not mean, however, that Peterson rejects the existence of evil qua evil. Evil, too, seems to constitute a fundamental part of reality, ontologically different from order and chaos yet potentially connected to both. I say "seems" because this, too, is an area of Peterson's thought that is challenging to pin down, especially given his frequent appeal to symbolism. For example, Peterson has this to say about hell:

> The idea that hell exists in some metaphysical manner is not only ancient, and pervasive; it's true. Hell is eternal. It has always existed. It exists now.[9]

That seems to suggest that evil is ontologically, and not just symbolically, real. Peterson, however, also suggests that Satan is not real per se, but rather represents the sum of all evil. In his meditations on the temptations of Christ, he writes, "Satan embodies the refusal of sacrifice; he is arrogance, incarnate; spite, deceit, and cruel, conscious malevolence. He is pure hatred of Man, God, and Being."[10] Hell, in other words, may exist metaphysically, but Satan is a "embodiment" of evil. To complexify things more, Peterson identifies Christ as the perfect man in an archetypal sense, but additionally suggests that evil also exists within him. Indeed, it is Christ's refusal to give into that evil that makes him the perfect man:

> [Christ is forever because] Christ is always he who is willing to confront evil—consciously, fully and voluntarily—in the form *that dwelt simultaneously within Him and in the world.* This is nothing merely abstract (although it is abstract); nothing to be brushed over. It is no intellectual matter.[11]

---

9. Peterson, *12 Rules for Life*, 220.
10. Peterson, 180.
11. Peterson, 180 (emphasis added). The attribution of evil to the nature of Christ is somewhat ambiguous here. Perhaps Peterson is referring to the temptation of Christ; however, the Christian tradition clearly holds that *uninvited* temptations themselves are not sinful, and so recognizing that Christ experiences temptation would not imply that he is sinning or has a disposition to sin. Rather, it emphasizes his *humanity.*

That perfection itself, represented in Christ, also contains evil generates an even more complicated metaphysical landscape. The ingredients up to this point are 1) order, 2) chaos, and 3) evil. Yet, as the Christ example additionally reveals, goodness, too, is in the mix (recall that order and chaos are not good or bad in and of themselves; they just *are*). Indeed, Peterson ultimately calls us to recognize that existence—"Being" in his words—is *more* good than evil in the final analysis. In his last rule, "Pet a cat whenever you see one on the street," he draws on Christ to observe, "Christ enjoins his followers to place faith in God's heavenly kingdom, and the truth. That's a conscious decision to presume the primary goodness of Being." That makes it appear, contrary to his claim that Christ contains evil, that Peterson associates Christ with pure ontological goodness. However, he seemingly pulls the rug from under that interpretation by stating one sentence later, "Aim high, like Pinocchio's Geppetto. Wish upon a star, and then act properly, in accordance with that aim."[12] So is the final goodness of Being a real Christ (Jesus) or a symbolic Christ (a "star" representing perfection)?

Save Yourself

I confess it is not clear to me how to pull all these strands—order, chaos, evil, goodness, symbolism, and existence—into a unified "Petersonian" metaphysics. What does emerge clearly, though, is that this metaphysical backdrop, Peterson's "Nature" with a big "N," forms the foundation for his response to how human beings are supposed to live. We already explored this theme in analyzing Peterson's understanding of meaning and its pursuit, but a few more important elements surface in this context.

The first is that Peterson interprets the metaphysical stew of Being described above not only as making suffering common and unavoidable; rather, he believes Being is tantamount to suffering. He writes,

---

12. Peterson, 351.

Take pain, for example—subjective pain. That's something so real no argument can stand against it. Everyone acts as if their pain is real—ultimately real. Pain matters, more than matter matters. It is for this reason, I believe, that so many of the world's traditions regard suffering attendant upon existence as the irreducible truth of Being.[13]

Suffering, in other words, is not only one more element in existence. It is the outcome of the sum total of the other elements. We therefore might say that chaos + order + evil + goodness = suffering = Being.

The only way to respond to existence so defined is, as Peterson puts it, "to raise up Being [suffering] on your shoulders where it belongs." This is the heart of his argument about pursuing what is meaningful rather than what is expedient. However, there is an additional dimension of Peterson's ethics now more visible: the solution to the problem of suffering, insofar as there is a solution, is to be found in the human will and the human will alone. This is additionally complicated because Peterson believes that the brokenness of the world is the consequence of the sum of broken individuals who fail to pursue meaning in their lives. The good news for Peterson, however, is that broken individuals have the power to fix themselves and, by extension, the world.

This principle of self-perfection lies at the foundation of rules four, "Compare yourself to who you were yesterday, not to someone else today," and six, "Set your house in perfect order before criticizing the world." It is not a naïve perfectionism; Peterson is too realistic about human nature to believe anyone could achieve perfection. However, he does seem to believe 1) that "better" can constantly move closer to "best" even if we never get there, and 2) the means by which we advance morally is by making ourselves better. As Peterson writes,

The present is eternally flawed. But where you start might not be as important as the direction you are heading. *Perhaps happiness is always to be*

---

13. Peterson, 35.

found in the journey uphill, and not in the fleeting satisfaction awaiting at the next peak. Much of happiness is hope, no matter how deep the underworld in which that hope was conceived. . . . Called upon properly, [your] internal critic will suggest something to set in order, which you *would* set in order—voluntarily, without resentment, even with pleasure.[14]

The right response to the suffering of existence, starting with the suffering in your own existence, is to work to make things better, starting with yourself, and, crucially, never stopping once you start. That is the significance of the "hill" metaphor. What it means to live meaningfully in a broken existence is to keep going up; what it means to keep going up is to make continual internal adjustments to fix the brokenness within so that, eventually, once your own house is in tolerable order, you can do something helpful to mitigate the suffering of those around you, of "the world." Indeed, for Peterson, that's the only way the world can be fixed and Being advanced. In a rare moment of optimism, Peterson writes about those who commit to clean up their own house:

> Perhaps you will discover that your now less-corrupted soul, much stronger than it might otherwise have been, is now able to bear those remaining, necessary, minimal, inescapable tragedies. . . . Perhaps your uncorrupted soul will then see its existence as a genuine good, as something to celebrate, even in the face of your own vulnerability. Perhaps you will become an ever-more-powerful force for peace and whatever is good. . . . Perhaps you will then see that if all people did this, in their own lives, the world might stop being an evil place. After that, with continued effort, perhaps it could even stop being a tragic place. . . . Who knows what eternal heavens might be established by our spirits, purified by truth, aiming skyward, right here on the fallen Earth?[15]

---

14. Peterson, 94.
15. Peterson, 159.

You are not only your own redeemer, your own savior, preaches Peterson. You should work to save yourself so that you can have a decent shot at saving others.

Back to the Garden

As with every other rule, the principles Peterson lays out in his conception of nature, Nature, and the proper human disposition to both overlap substantially with foundational Christian principles. For example, Christianity tends to view little "n" nature the same way as Peterson, recognizing that nature both constitutes a fixed entity whose rules we must respect yet is also open to interpretation. On the question of gender ideology, for example, the Magisterium of the Catholic Church (meaning it's official teaching authority) recently released a document firmly rejecting the claim that human beings have the capacity to "choose" their own gender or to alter their biological sex.[16] Indeed, recognizing the fixedness of nature, including human nature, is at the heart of Catholic teaching on how to understand the world and humanity's place within it. Contrary to popular prejudices (not helped by forms of Christianity that employ an exclusively literalistic interpretation of the Bible—which is a nonbiblical interpretive principle!), most Christians see no conflict between scientific and biblical interpretations of reality properly defined. Indeed, Pope St. John Paul II issued a document during his papacy affirming potential truths in evolutionary theory so long as the theory is located within a broader philosophically and theologically consistent understanding of existence and its source.[17] This may come as news to the secular world, but it is not surprising theologically. If there is one God, as Christians hold, then there must be one creation, which means, in

---

16. See Congregation for Catholic Education, *"Male and Female He Created Them": Towards a Path of Dialogue on the Question of Gender Theory in Education*, Higher Education of the Catholic Church: Congregation for Catholic Education, February 2, 2019, http://www.educatio.va/content/dam/cec/Documenti/19_0997_INGLESE.pdf.

17. See Pope John Paul II, "Message to the Pontifical Academy of Sciences: On Evolution," Smithsonian National Museum of Natural History: What Does It Mean to Be Human?, October 22, 1996, https://humanorigins.si.edu/.

an ultimate sense, everything must emerge from the same source. Explaining the process by which the emergence and development of life takes place is a question scientific analysis can greatly contribute to without threatening any philosophical and theological truth. In this sense, Christianity substantively, if not completely, embraces both Peterson's methodology and conclusions as they relate to little "n" nature: there is an objective nature that provides that basic structure for how human beings ought to live, including how we understand what it means to be female and male.

The Christian tradition also recognizes humanity and nature in a relationship of interpretation, a "dance" in Peterson's metaphor. Indeed, interpreting nature, "humanizing" it, lies at the heart of the creation account in Genesis: "Out of the ground the LORD God formed every animal of the field and every bird of the air, and he brought them to the man to see what he would call them; and whatever the man called every living creature, that was its name" (Gen. 2:19). God creates, we name. That is the dance at the heart of the biblical conception of humanity's relationship with nature. Nature is not ours to create; it has an objective existence that precedes us. However, God does give us the power to name, and that name becomes a part of the natural world itself. We therefore *are* creatures with fixed natures in a fixed natural landscape from the Christian standpoint; however, we are not slaves to nature, an insight also captured in God giving human beings "dominion," now often translated as "stewardship," over nature in Genesis (see Gen. 1:26). On this, there is agreement with Peterson as well.

Where Christianity departs from Peterson, however, is on his metaphysics—Nature with a big "N." This divergence is not only at the level of abstract metaphysical principles; the differences also have profound ethical implications on how individuals should live in relation to themselves, others, and existence more broadly. Peterson, recall, identifies different opposing causal forces at work in Nature: order, chaos, goodness, and evil. Suffering and pain are the product of these forces clashing—which Peterson calls "Being"—and the right response to Being so-defined is to *advance* Being by reducing the degree to which suffering constitutes it. The *means* by which that is accomplished is by individuals choosing to "clean up" their own houses by embracing meaning over expediency. The collective outcome of this individual work can, if enough people do it, lead to a collective diminishment of suffering, which is tantamount to the advancement of Being for all.

Again, if I am describing Peterson accurately, I find this confluence of claims about reality confusing. For example, how can suffering both define Being while the reduction of suffering advances it? *Where* is Being going (what potential is it realizing?), and what is the name of the reality to which Being should ultimately conform? If chaos and order are coequal forces, what meta-force governs the balance between them? Likewise, how can good and evil coexist as both real without locating their source in two competing "divinities" of some kind?

However Peterson might answer these questions, the biblical tradition sees things very differently. First, there are no primordial opposing forces at work in Nature. There is only God, who is not one being among many but rather, as St. Thomas Aquinas puts it, Being itself. God is uniquely noncontingent, meaning he (using the biblical language) does not depend on any other being for his existence. God is also simple, meaning he is not made up of component parts (the Holy Trinity does not describe different "parts" of God but rather God being in relation to himself). Second, the biblical God chooses to create the universe, the material world and everything in it. This means both that God transcends the world yet is also intimately related to everything in the world as its Creator and sustainer. Third, God chooses to create human beings within the world according to his image and likeness, which means that humans share in God's nature 1) by having a rational, immaterial soul, and 2) by possessing the capacities of reason and free will.

It is crucial to emphasize that everything, without exception, is good within creation, including human beings and their unique capacities. God, in Genesis, recognizes that that which he has created is "good" after each day of creation, and he gives the designation of "very good" to the creation of human beings. That means that evil, pain, and suffering are not real in an absolute sense, a point Bishop Barron has also repeatedly emphasized in his work.[18] There is thus no corner of the universe in which evil, in any form, naturally exists, no primordial portal through which darkness pours in. In fact, darkness isn't real at all. There is only light, God's light, refracted in innumerable diversity throughout creation and culminating in human beings. Likewise, there is no duality, no chaos-eating-order-eating-chaos that constitutes a cosmic balance between competing forces. There is only one God, and, as one, God cannot oppose either himself or his creation. This "cannot" applies both in the metaphysical sense (there being one God implies there is no possible source of opposition) and, consequently, in the motivational sense as well: given that creation is good—which it must be since it is created by God—there is no theological rationale why God would act against that which God has created. The *shema* of Israel beautifully encapsulates this theological vision: "Hear, O Israel: The LORD is our God, the LORD alone" (Deut. 6:4). This one God, again as Bishop Barron has frequently taught, is not in competition with existence. He does not work against that which he has created.

But that which he has created can work against him, in the form of human sin. The Christian conception of sin also deviates profoundly from Peterson's account. Peterson interprets the fall of humanity—the first sin—as human beings becoming aware of their mortality and of the existence of evil within themselves. He writes, for example, *"Evil enters the world with self-consciousness."*[19] He further explains, meditating on Adam and Eve:

> Once you become consciously aware that you, yourself, are vulnerable, you understand the nature of human vulnerability, in general. You understand what it's like to be fearful, and angry, and resentful, and bitter. You understand what pain means. And once you truly understand such feelings

---

18. See, for example, Bishop Robert Barron, "Pain Is Not Metaphysically Basic," Word on Fire, April 18, 2019, https://www.wordonfire.org/resources/article/pain-is-not-metaphysically-basic/23992/.
19. Peterson, *12 Rules for Life*, 176.

in yourself, and how they are produced, *you understand how to produce them in others.* It is in this manner that the self-conscious beings that we are become voluntarily and exquisitely capable of tormenting others (and ourselves).[20]

Note here that Peterson implies that self-consciousness becomes aware of something that was already there in humanity—namely, a primordial seed of destruction containing a latent desire to harm others and oneself. Self-consciousness only activates that capacity. In other words, Peterson interprets the fall as the event in which human beings recognize their potential for evil, not create it.

Christianity sees the fall very differently, for reasons that should already be apparent in the description of creation itself. If there is one God, and God, by definition, is all good, then everything that God creates must, by metaphysical necessity, be all good as well. That is precisely what we see in Genesis' account of creation: everything is good, including human nature, including *every* human being by nature. There is, in other words, no latent evil in human beings, no bad seed that gets activated at the dawn of self-awareness. This inherent goodness includes the human capacities for knowledge and freedom as well: from a biblical perspective, there is nothing about the act of knowing (including self-awareness) or the exercise of freedom that implies evil. Nothing. Indeed, that is the significance of God telling humanity in Genesis that they are *free* to eat of any of the other trees in the garden. This use of freedom, and the attendant capacity to understand what it means to choose among the different "trees," is part of the goodness of creation itself.

Yet what about the one tree that God prohibits, the tree of the knowledge of good and evil that is located next to the tree of life in the middle of the garden? Doesn't that mean that evil does already exist as part of creation and, moreover, that God is tempting humans to become evil by placing it in

---

20. Peterson, 174–175.

the garden with all the other trees? No. It is crucial to recognize that the tree is not the "tree of good and evil," as if it represents a metaphysical duality already present in creation. Rather, it is the tree of the *knowledge* of good and evil. As such, the tree itself, like everything else in the garden, is good. But how, then, can evil be known if it does not already exist? And how can we not pin at least some of the blame on God for the existence of evil, since he put the tree there in the first place?

The Problem of Sin

Here's one way of addressing these questions by appealing to basic Christian theological anthropology. Human beings, in their naturally created state, are free to choose among the goods that naturally exist in creation. This is genuine freedom. In exercising this freedom, they are also freely choosing to obey the one command of God: "And the LORD God commanded the man, 'You may freely eat of every tree of the garden; but of the tree of the knowledge of good and evil you shall not eat, for in the day that you eat of it you shall die'" (Gen. 2:16–17). Obeying this command is electing, again freely, to live in accordance with goodness itself, life itself, God himself, insofar as God is the creator of all that is.

However, that same freedom to choose goodness in obedience to God's command necessarily implies the freedom to do the opposite, the freedom to disobey. What would disobeying look like? If everything in existence is good, then the only "thing" we could possibly choose in disobeying God commands would be "no-thing" or nothing itself, absence itself, nullity itself, sheer vacuity of existence—nonbeing, in other words—and *nonbeing is the same "thing" as death*: to choose against God is to choose *for* death. It is for this reason we see God warning the first humans in Genesis, "For the day you eat of it you shall die." The "no" to God necessarily entails, metaphysically, a "yes" to death, because that is the only other "thing" we could possibly choose in rejecting God and God's creation (i.e., "all the trees of the garden"). In other words, the story of the fall is the story of

God giving everything to human beings and human beings replying, "We want more than everything; *we want nothing as well.*" And because we are free, God let us have it.

But that does not mean God is responsible for death, sin, and evil. God created human freedom, which is good. But human freedom, qua human freedom, has the real possibility to act against God—which is to say, to act against its own source. That is what the *knowledge* of good and evil in the tree points to. It's not that humans don't have any knowledge before the fall. They know the good intimately. In, fact, it's all they know; prior to the fall, evil can't be known because it is not an object existing in the external world. It only "exists" in the sense of a potentiality, a potentiality that only human freedom can bring into existence by disobeying the command of God. Thus, in the act of disobedience, we not only come to know evil; we concomitantly create that which is known.[21] And, in this sense, we do something even God cannot do: generate nothingness, the absence of what *is*.

Two analogies may help illustrate. First, St. Augustine consistently describes evil as "nothingness" and sin as a "lie." This doesn't only mean that telling lies is a sin, though Augustine believes that is the case. His deeper point is that evil and sin itself, in its totality, is a lie. The reason is because lies are, by nature, parasitic on the truth. Truth can exist without lies. It just *is*. However, a lie, by definition, *depends* on the existence of truth for its own existence. For a lie to be effective in tricking someone, the lie must be taken to be true. A lie parasitically feeds off the truth to come into existence. Yet at the same time, a lie doesn't exist because that's precisely what a lie is: nonbeing, nonexistence, pointing to something that really isn't there. A lie, in other words, tears a hole in the fabric of existence by using existence itself to create a nothingness.

---

21. It is important to note that the serpent in the story is usually interpreted as the presence of the devil in creation. God did not create the devil, though he did create angels. Christianity understands the devil, and demons more broadly, as angels who employed their reason and free will to definitively reject God, a decision God permits the angels to make. Note that the serpent can only *tempt* humans to sin; he cannot force them to. This highlights the freedom of their decision to turn away from God.

The fall, then, the story of the first sin, is the story of the first lie. In disobeying God's command, humans use the goodness of existence to create the absence of existence. They use life to create death. God's prohibition of eating of the tree of the knowledge of good and evil thus has nothing to do with control over human beings or imposing his sovereignty over their freedom. The opposite is the case: the command—and this is always the case in the Bible—is meant to protect human freedom, to protect our ability both to know and to choose the good, which is the same as choosing life.

A second analogy helps explain why that is the case. Bishop Barron has frequently employed the metaphor of "addiction" to describe the nature of sin. It is particularly apt in the context of interpreting the fall. An addiction is a deep attachment to something that harms you, indeed, destroys you. Think, for example, of the opioid epidemic in the United States. The most recent death tolls are staggering—over 60,000 people overdosed in one year. How can that be? This is a separate number from suicides; presumably, the people who overdose don't consciously want to die. And yet they kill themselves anyway, injecting poison into their blood. With every addiction story, we can imagine an alternative scenario in which the same person could have carried on life without the poison. In fact, the poison is poison because it doesn't belong there, doesn't need to be there, would never had been missed if it had never been discovered.

The fall is the story of humanity's first hit of the hardest, most addictive drug there is: pride. It's not only the act of disobedience itself that is thrilling. It's also the fact that the act was, in a perverted sense, godlike: in rejecting the true God, they *create* something new, something that had never been before in the universe. This is the dark rush of both the meth-head and the meth-maker in one: we make the mix and then hit it hard. And then: "The eyes of both were opened" (Gen. 3:7).

Let me appeal to parents to explain what is going on in the text. Mothers and fathers, when you have a child, you ideally do so, not because you lack something and need to fill it but rather out of a superabundance of love. Life begets life, ideally, out of this kind of love. In that new creation, you make something that is *of* you but also different from you. You are responsible for the child but would never think of the child as your property or yours do with as you wish. Indeed, the only thing you want for the child is for her or him to be happy, authentically happy, to grow into the kind of person who can give and receive love, the kind of person who can continue the cycle of life by becoming a good parent, producing new life with the same love.

So what you do you teach your child with this singular aim in mind? You say things like: "I want you, my dear one, to experience all the good this world has to offer. I want you to mark your own path, to discover your own way of being; I want you to become everything I know you can become." And because you say things like that, you also say things like this: "Because I love you, because I want you to be happy, I ask that you *never ever* _____." Now that "never ever" could potentially include many things, but perhaps we can agree that one of those things should be this: "Never try methamphetamines; because I love you, never ever try methamphetamines." But as you say this, purely out of love and not out of a desire to control, you also know that you cannot prevent your children from taking that path if that is the path they choose to take. They are young now, but they will grow; and as they grow, their freedom and sense of self will blossom, and they will make their own choices. So you do everything you can in the meantime. You give them every good experience you can possibly give them, showing them the beauty of a life well lived. And you warn them of the dangers of straying too far off the well-marked paths. You warn them not to go into the dark. And they trust you because that's what children do.

But then one night, a peer approaches and says to your child who is no longer a child, "Did your parents tell you not to 'party'? That is only because they are old and jealous of you and don't want you to have any fun; it's only because they are scared you will make your own choices and be your own person; it's only because they want to have power over you. Come; I want to show you something." And, God forbid, your child follows, hesitantly but with a growing sense of rebellion. The bedroom door opens, and there it is: the spoon, the needle, and the flame, surrounded by the blissful smiles of youthful faces, each beckoning your child come closer. And he does. She does. It is all a delight for the senses: the low lights, the soft music, the magical haze of smoke, and bodies in pleasurable repose. The hesitation fades and resolve wells up: *I am my own damn person.* Then the consent and the dark delight of its recognition as the band is tied and the skin is penetrated. And the eyes are opened.

We know, fellow parents, that if this happens, or if it has already happened, there is no going back to innocence for our children. In the best-case scenario, the man or woman doesn't become an overt addict, with all the horrors that entails. In the best-case scenario, the man or woman doesn't use again. That would be fantastic, of course. But even if that's possible, every day after the first hit will have to be a struggle. Doing what is right—not injecting poison in your veins—will be a fight. What used to be so natural, so easy—getting out of bed without thinking about drugs, taking a shower without thinking about drugs, going to work without thinking about drugs, eating meals without thinking about drugs—will become constant toil, require constant labor. That's what happens when you lose your innocence. It's not that you get kicked out of the garden. It's that you literally can't see it anymore. Your open eyes make you blind to paradise.

So why don't we just stop our children from taking this path? Why don't we just force them not to destroy themselves? We know the answer immediately: because our children are free, and we want them to be free. That is the tragedy. The same thing that makes love possible can be used to break your heart.

This analogy has limits, of course, but it gets at the fundamental problem of sin from a biblical perspective: we are made from life for life and given everything possible to choose the path of life. But just like Adam and Eve, we take our first hit of pride, of the poison of creating nonbeing, and become addicted, which, in turn, creates the fundamental theological dilemma: How can God help us get out of our addiction without taking away our freedom?

Much of the Old Testament can be interpreted as attempted answers to that question. You can try starting over (Noah), you can try by focusing on a small group of people whose holiness will attract all humanity back to the source of life (Abraham), you can offer the people laws that, if they follow them, will keep them on the path of life (Moses), you can guide the people to the establishment of a community that marks the unity of heaven and earth and serves as a light beckoning all back to their true home (David). But what happens every time in an almost comic consistency is that we not only look these gift horses in the mouth. We knock out their teeth just for the hell of it. We throw the pearls before swine. We gild lilies one moment, desiccate them with neglect the next, and then stomp on them, annoyed by their beauty.

This is the problem of sin from the Christian perspective. The fall in Genesis captures its origins. The rest of the Bible, up to and through the Crucifixion of Christ, narrates the consequences. Sin is not only "missing the mark," as Peterson calls it. It is also hating the mark while hating oneself for hating the mark. As St. Paul writes in his Letter to the Romans, "I do not understand my own actions. For I do not do what I want, but I do the very thing I hate. Now if I do what I do not want, I agree that the law is good. But in fact it is no longer I that do it, but sin that dwells within me. . . . I can will what is right, but I cannot do it. For I do not do the good I want, but the evil I do not want is what I do" (Rom. 7:15–19).

"I can will what is right, but I cannot do it." *That* is the problem of sin: being the cause of your own destruction, knowing that you are the cause of your own destruction, not wanting to be the cause of your own destruction—as you destroy yourself.

Amazing Grace

In the end, the reason it's so important to get the metaphysics right is not to score some theoretical victory over rival conceptions of reality. It's because metaphysics are eminently practical: how you define reality itself will ultimately define how you define your reality, and how you define your reality will ultimately define how you live your life—and how you live your life will determine, well, everything. Inadequate metaphysics equates to unhappy people.

153

With all respect to Peterson's brilliance, his metaphysics ultimately work against his primary goal in writing *12 Rules*—helping people to reduce suffering—because they lead them in the wrong direction: back only to themselves. It's not that the Christian tradition disagrees with the rule to set your own house in order before criticizing others or to compare yourself to who you were yesterday rather than other people today. Indeed, it happily endorses those rules in the form of, as we see in the thought of St. Thomas Aquinas, for example, defining the Christian life according to seven virtues: temperance, fortitude, justice, and prudence (the natural moral virtues), and faith, hope, and love (the supernatural virtues). For Aquinas, it is impossible either to attain individual salvation or to improve the world without these virtues. We have also seen previously how much the biblical tradition condemns people who seek to fix others while living in brokenness themselves.

Rather, where Christianity fundamentally departs from Peterson is in *how* following these rules is possible in the first place. Locating human beings within a landscape of waring powers, one in which evil, to some degree, is real like truth, in which chaos and order fight like jealous deities over human allegiance, in which the fundamental reality of suffering in existence renders all of us, at best, like Sisyphuses rolling stones of responsibility up hills, waiting for them to topple back over us so that we can roll them up again, as the world turns in rote revolutions of pain—these are not the ingredients of a noble adventure. Adventures are filled with dangers, deadly dangers, but also the possibility of real victory, of an *end* to the fighting in the form of winning the lasting peace. It's not only the case that Peterson's metaphysics have philosophical inconsistencies. It's that those inconsistencies, when applied to human life, make for an adventure whose endings can only be tragic or slightly less than tragic. That's not an adventure. That's only marginally better than a nightmare.

Here's the Christian alternative. In the realm of the natural, we get to preserve the laws of nature, recognizing that they offer us the most basic patterns for our flourishing, and therefore, we only abandon them at our peril. However, we also recognize that we are more than the biological dictates of our nature; as creatures with rational souls, we engage with our nature as a partner in being, not a master, and, in so doing, expand the horizon of the good beyond the natural.

At the level of big "N" Nature, we recognize there are, indeed, meta-patterns that govern the laws of nature. But rather than attributing them to a cosmic duality of chaos and order, we see them as governed by a single power that works through existence, throughout creation, in manifold diversity, a power that can appear chaotic but is, in fact, always rational, always tied to the Logos, the divine reason, the, in Aquinas' words, eternal law. From this theocentric perspective, goodness is the only authentic existence, and the only deviation from it comes as a result of sin entering the world by human hands—not because God willed that sin become a shadow part of reality but rather because he permitted it. And he permitted it only because he created humans with a free will, and the condition for the possibility of being able to choose the good is being able to reject the good.

Sin entering the world creates great suffering, individually and socially, physically, mentally, and spiritually. Pain is present everywhere, hidden and unhidden. However, pain does not have the last word, because it did not have the first word. Like Peterson, Christianity calls human beings to do every-thing in their power to "clean up their own" houses both externally, in their actions, and internally, in their attitudes, dispositions, and even thoughts. We are called to be good people, not just to do good things. To the extent that it is possible, this ongoing house cleaning, ongoing dedication to moral improvement, will yield good fruit. Things will not be as bad as they could have been. Some progress toward virtue will be made if we're responsible and persistent.

But we will fail. We will always fail. We intend to do what is right, but do not do it. Or do what is right, but do not will it (like doing a good deed for the benefit of praise). We'll have a week of stellar good behavior and buoyant smiles and blow it all up in five seconds of seething hate toward someone we buy anniversary gifts for. We'll give fantastic advice and not abide by an ounce of it. We'll engage in the grossest forms of hypocrisy, disgusted to see in others what we have been silently massaging in ourselves for years. We'll do public acts of charity while secretly suspecting that our lives are probably worth more than our neighbors, or, at least, some of our neighbors, at least the disheveled and dirty ones. All things considered, to the extent we believe in God beyond saying that we do (or saying that we might), we are sure, just sure, that we're going to heaven—if, that is, there is a heaven. Because, after all, how could someone like me deserve anything else? I mean: *it's me*.

That's the problem with sin, the problem with having a taste for sweet pride-dipped death. No matter how hard we try to be good, we're never really going *to be* good. That's not an indictment of the good. It's an indictment of us. We broke it, but we can't fix it, even if we take responsibility for trying (which we should). Since we are the cause of the problem, we cannot also be the solution, at least not a lasting solution. Is there any evidence otherwise? If we could fix ourselves, if we could make ourselves whole, then why all the books, all the videos, all the conferences, all the therapy, all the apps, all the cross-legged breathing, all the pills? Just fix yourself and be done already! Just tell the addict to stop getting high *and* wanting to get high and then do it!

But we can't—not on our own. We can be a worthy opponent to death perhaps (and that is a big perhaps), but not a victor. Nobody beats death.

Well, almost nobody.

This is where things get good, where Peterson's path and the Christian's path really start to diverge. Christians don't believe Jesus is just a moral exemplar or an archetypal standard of perfection. Christians believe he is God incarnate, the living God made flesh— human in every dimension except for sin. The Gospels are adamant about this: Jesus is the Lord, God among us. He is fully a man, and he is fully God. And who does this man reveal God to be? Whatever specific answers we may give in describing the identity of the Christ, all of them, ultimately, must be synthesized in the cross: God is the God who not only freely suffers for us but he who dies for us. *God dies for you*.

Why God would do that doesn't make sense unless we return to the nature of sin. Sin, recall, is death; it is the turning inside out of reality and making a lie out of a truth. We are responsible for its existence, but, like artificial intelligence programmers who write a code that gets out of control and takes over the programmers, we can't undo what we've done. Even our efforts to fight sin become tainted with sin. And so God, Christians believe, in an act of divine love first inaugurated in creation but consummated in the cross, does what human beings cannot do: he absorbs death, the sin of the world, into his very body, sucking in every form of cruelty, every form of hatred, every form of delight in another's misfortune, every cutting, backstabbing quip—the whole range of evil—into his very self, and he dies death, all the way down, even into, as Bishop Barron has observed, godforsakenness itself, which we see captured in Jesus' heartrending lines while dying on the cross, "My God, My God, why have you forsaken me?" (Matt. 27:46). Then he dies. Really dies.

But then he comes back to life. Really comes back to life. And what that means is that life, not death, has the final word. Life, not death, is the most fundamental characteristic of existence. Life, not death, is the culmination of God's creation and God's activity in the world. God liberates his people, and we are all his people.

But, of course, we're still free. God in and through Jesus Christ creates the conditions for redemption. He establishes himself as the bridge to the fullness of life. Yet we must choose to cross the bridge, to walk the path of life back to the author of life. God's not going to do that for us. He loves us, after all, and love always respects freedom, or it is not love.

Here's the good news though. If you do make the choice to cross, you will never walk alone. You will fall, slip backward. You will walk slowly, even crawl. You will be assailed and mocked. You may even have to start over, perhaps start over several times. So be it. It doesn't matter, not in an ultimate sense. God's mercy, St. Faustina wrote, is like an ocean. You cannot deplete it, cannot dry it out, cannot sin one too many times. Provided that you are willing to get back up (with help) and return to the path, there isn't a "too many" times.

That is the authentic adventure of life—full of danger, full of pain, full of suffering, full of periods of darkness, to be sure. But also full of such wonder that it hurts; such joy that you can hardly keep yourself together (because you no longer want to); such peace that you question whether depression is even possible; such gratitude that you feel the only proper response is to make everything in your life about sharing the gift of grace with anyone who will listen. That's real too. And it's accessible to everyone, on two conditions: "Love the Lord your God with all your heart, and with all your soul, and with all your strength, and with all your mind; and your neighbor as yourself" (Luke 10:27).

Two rules for life from the Lord of life, who offers us eternal life.

EPILOGUE

A Christian Response to *Beyond Order*

Christopher Kaczor and Matthew R. Petrusek

EPILOGUE

Suffering and the Story of Life

Beyond Order: 12 More Rules for Life begins with stories of extraordinary suffering. Peterson details the horrific suffering of his wife, Tammy, who was given a diagnosis of terminal cancer and nearly died on multiple occasions but was rescued as if by miracle from the brink of death. Jordan's own misery included witnessing his beloved wife's sufferings, contracting COVID-19, acute sleeplessness, double pneumonia, crippling anxiety, severe side effects of anti-anxiety medications, even more severe side effects of withdrawing from these medications, and overwhelming thoughts of self-destruction. On the opening page of *Beyond Order*, he vividly describes waking up in an intensive care ward in Moscow with no memory of the weeks prior:

> I had six-inch tethers attaching me to the sides of the bed because, in my unconscious state, I had been agitated enough to try to remove the catheters from my arm and leave the ICU. I was confused and frustrated not knowing where I was, surrounded by people speaking a foreign language, and in the absence of my daughter, Mikhaila, and her husband, Andrey, who were restricted to short visiting hours and did not have permission to be there with me at my moment of wakening. I was angry, too, about being there, and lunged at my daughter when she did visit several hours later. I felt betrayed, although that was the furthest from the truth.[1]

Their whole family went through a kind of living hell. No one who lives long has a life without suffering. But Jordan Peterson, his wife, Tammy, and their

---

1. Jordan Peterson, *Beyond Order: 12 More Rules for Life* (New York: Portfolio, 2021), xv.

daughter, Mikhaila, have had much, much more suffering than many. What was it that enabled Peterson to get through this suffering? Peterson writes,

> I can tell you what has saved me, so far—the love I have for my family; the love they have for me; the encouragement they have delivered, along with my friends; the fact that I still had meaningful work I could struggle through while in the abyss.[2]

The story of Jordan Peterson is, in its own way, a rearticulation of the story of the eternal romance, the story of love enabling endurance of suffering. The triumph of love over death goes by way of suffering. "The cross, for its part, is the burden of life," writes Peterson. "It is a place of betrayal, torture, and death. It is therefore a fundamental symbol of mortal vulnerability. In the Christian drama, it is also the place where vulnerability is transcended, as a consequence of its acceptance."[3] Each one of us has our own cross. Whatever it is, and whoever we are, we cannot escape that cross.

The inevitable suffering of our lives leads us to ask questions. Some of these questions can be answered by scientific research, but empirical investigation also leaves many of our questions unanswered. Who am I? Where have I come from? Where am I going?

Science Is Not Enough

Such queries cannot fully be answered by science. We answer them in part by knowing ourselves, and we know ourselves and those we love through stories. Peterson writes,

> Get your story straight. Past, present, future—they all matter. You need to map your path. You need to know where you were, so that you do not repeat the mistakes of the past. You need to know where you are, or you

---

2. Peterson, xxiii.
3. Peterson, 75.

will not be able to draw a line from your starting point to your destination. You need to know where you are going, or you will drown in uncertainty, unpredictability, and chaos, and starve for hope and inspiration. For better or worse, you are on a journey.[4]

Peterson holds that our own individual stories are enmeshed with and cannot be properly understood apart from the stories of those in our lives. In this, he echoes the Catholic convert, philosopher Alasdair MacIntyre: "I am part of their story, as they are part of mine. The narrative of any one life is part of an interlocking set of narratives."[5] In our everyday decisions, we are writing in deeds the story of our lives and contributing to the stories of all those whose lives we touch, especially our families. And these individual and family stories are themselves fractals of bigger stories of clan, country, and culture.[6] Regardless of who we are as individuals in all our particularity, we are part of stories larger than ourselves. As McIntyre said,

> Man is in his actions and practice, as well as in his fictions, essentially a story-telling animal. He is not essentially, but becomes through his history, a teller of stories that aspire to truth. But the key question for men is not about their own authorship; I can only answer the question "What am I to do?" if I can answer the prior question "Of what story or stories do I find myself a part?" We enter human society, that is, with one or more imputed characters—roles into which we have been drafted—and we have to learn what they are in order to be able to understand how others respond to us and how our responses to them are apt to be construed. It is through hearing stories about wicked step-mothers, lost children, good but misguided kings, wolves that suckle twin boys, youngest sons who receive no inheritance but must make their own way in the world and eldest sons

---

4. Peterson, 86.

5. Alasdair MacIntyre, *After Virtue: A Study in Moral Theory*, 3rd ed. (Notre Dame: University of Notre Dame Press, 2007), 218.

6. Eleonore Stump, *Wandering in Darkness: Narrative and the Problem of Suffering* (New York: Oxford University Press, 2010), ch. 3.

who waste their inheritance on riotous living and go into exile to live with the swine, that children learn or mislearn both what a child and what a parent is, what the cast of characters may be in the drama into which they have been born and what the ways of the world are. Deprive children of stories and you leave them unscripted, anxious stutterers in their actions as in their words. Hence there is no way to give us an understanding of any society, including our own, except through the stock of stories which constitute its initial dramatic resources. Mythology, in its original sense, is at the heart of things. Vico was right and so was Joyce. And so too of course is that moral tradition from heroic society to its medieval heirs according to which the telling of stories has a key part in educating us into the virtues.[7]

These stories are not scientific descriptions of who we are as material beings, but we should not reject them on that account. There are more things in heaven and earth, to paraphrase Shakespeare, than are dreamt of in empirical science. Peterson writes,

It is also by no means self-evident that value, subjective though it appears to be, is not an integral part of reality, despite the undeniable utility of the scientific method. The central scientific axiom left to us by the Enlightenment—that reality is the exclusive domain of the objective—poses a fatal challenge to the reality of religious experience, if the latter experience is fundamentally subjective (and it appears to be exactly that). But there is something complicating the situation that seems to lie between the subjective and the objective. What if there are experiences that typically manifest themselves to one person at a time (as seems to be the case with much of revelation), but appear to form a meaningful pattern when considered collectively? That indicates something is occurring that is not merely subjective, even though it cannot be easily pinned down with the existing

7. MacIntyre, After Virtue, 216.

methods of science. It could be, instead, that the value of something is sufficiently idiosyncratic—sufficiently dependent on the particularities of time, place, and the individual experiencing that thing—that it cannot be fixed and replicated in the manner required for it to exist as a scientific object. This does not mean, however, that value is not real: It means only that it is so complex that it cannot yet and may never fit itself within the scientific worldview.[8]

It is reasonable to recognize realities that cannot be scientifically verified. If we are consistent, we should reject the chief claim of *scientism*. Scientism claims that reality is the exclusive domain of the objectively, scientifically, empirically verified. But this claim is itself not objectively, scientifically, empirically verified. Scientism, the belief that we should only believe what science shows to be true, is not confirmed by science. So religious experience is unendangered by scientism, since scientism is a fatally flawed, self-defeating belief. But even if scientism were not self-defeating, it is clear, as Peterson points out, that science alone does not give us full access to reality.

Knowledge of Persons

Imagine a scientist, a hundred years from now, who has deep scientific knowledge of your mother obtained through studying her medical records. The scientist knows her height, weight, blood pressure, fingerprints, DNA, and family tree to the fifth generation. In some ways, the scientist knows more about your mother than you do. But in other important ways, you know much more about your mother than any scientist ever will. You know how she smells, how she feels, and what brought tears to her eyes. You remember her expression and her tone of voice when she told you that your grandfather died. You know whether she's trustworthy, whether she is kind, and whether she loves you. None of that knowledge has been scientifically

---

8. Peterson, *Beyond Order,* 165.

verified in double-blind studies set in laboratory conditions. But the knowledge you have of your mother is real, and this knowledge is characteristically much more important than knowing about her fingerprints or her DNA. The scientist scientifically knows your mother, but you personally know your mother.

The philosopher Eleonore Stump distinguishes between Dominican knowledge (scientific, impersonal, logical, philosophical, knowledge *about*) and Franciscan knowledge (non-scientific, personal, intuitive, narrative, personal knowledge *of*).[9] Both kinds of knowledge are important and real. However, when we want to know about persons, Franciscan knowledge is characteristically more important. If someone says to you, "Tell me about your mother," it is unlikely that you'll recite facts drawn from her medical records. You'll talk about your mother's character, and you might convey the most important information by stories that illustrate who she is.

God works in a similar way. Thomas Aquinas and other philosophers hold that we can have true knowledge of God by means of reason, logic, and philosophy. Thomas famously offered the "five ways" to argue for the existence of God.[10] But God reveals himself most fully not in philosophical arguments but in the person of Jesus of Nazareth. And the story of Jesus brings us to the beginning, when the eternal Word spoke creation into existence.

In the Bible, the story of the whole human race and of the creation of the universe itself begins with Genesis. Peterson writes,

There is an ethical claim deeply embedded in the Genesis account of creation: everything that emerges from the realm of possibility in the act of creation (arguably, either divine or human) is good insofar as the motive for its creation is good.[11]

9. Stump, *Wandering in Darkness*, 39–81.
10. Thomas Aquinas, *Summa theologiae* 1.2.3.
11. Peterson, *Beyond Order*, 260.

But *why* is the motive for creation good? In some ancient accounts like the speech of Aristophanes in Plato's *Symposium*, the gods make human beings solely for the purpose of serving the gods. The divine motive for creation is selfish. By contrast, according to St. Thomas Aquinas, God's motive for creation in general and of human beings in particular is radically unselfish, unforced generosity. God is not, as in Star Wars, like the Force, with a light side and a dark side, a generous side and a selfish side. God alone is perfectly good in every respect, having no admixture of evil. Moreover, God cannot benefit from what he does because God is absolutely perfect, requiring nothing from anyone else to make him become perfect. So when God gives, it is not to make God better but for the sake of those to whom God gives. Since to love is to give to others for their own sake, and this is exactly what God does in creation, Aquinas concludes that God is love.[12]

But even before creation, it was true that God is love. In the *Divine Comedy,* the poet Dante described God as the "First Love."[13] From all eternity God the Father loved God the Son, and God the Son loved God the Father. The Holy Spirit is the love between Father and Son. From this first family of love, God chose to give the gift of creation, including the creation of human persons who were, like God, able of love. Pseudo-Dionysius taught that goodness is diffusive of itself, so God, the highest good—the Good itself—motivated by love, created free human beings so that this goodness could be more widely shared. If creation arises from and reflects the First Love, then creation is good, very good.

Law, Love, and Happiness

Yet the abundant goodness of creation is insufficient for us to live in splendid isolation. As Peterson puts it,

---

12. Thomas Aquinas, *Summa theologiae* 1.20.1; *Summa contra Gentiles* 1.91, trans. Anton Pegis (New York: Hanover House, 1955), updated by Joseph Kenny, OP, https://isidore.co/aquinas/english/ContraGentiles.htm.

13. Dante, *Paradiso* 6.11, in *The Divine Comedy*, trans. Frederick Pollock (London: Chapman and Hall, 1854), 412.

We must perceive and act in a manner that meets our biological and psychological needs—but, since none of us lives or can live in isolation, we must meet them in a manner approved of by others. This means that the solutions we apply to our fundamental biological problems must also be acceptable and implementable socially. . . . The fact of limited solutions implies the existence of something like a natural ethic—variable, perhaps, as human languages are variable, but still characterized by something solid and universally recognizable at its base.[14]

What Peterson calls a natural ethic is what earlier thinkers in the Catholic tradition, including Thomas Aquinas, called the natural law. Indeed, Peterson's explanation is a rearticulation of MacIntyre's account of natural law. MacIntyre writes,

What then is it to know the natural law, if we are functioning normally and developing in a way that at least approximates our ideal development? . . . To inquire of ourselves and of each other "What is my good? What is our common good?" and to answer these questions by our actions and our practices as much as by our judgments. The life that expresses our shared human nature is a life of practical inquiry and practical reasoning, and we cannot but presuppose the precepts of the natural law in asking and answering those fundamental questions through our everyday activities and practices.[15]

In order to reason successfully about our good as individuals or our good in community, we must be in dialogue with one another.

What then are the necessary conditions for the possibility of any successful dialogue? For MacIntyre, echoing Thomas Aquinas, the preconditions for

---

14. Peterson, *Beyond Order*, 10.
15. Alasdair MacIntyre, "Theories of Natural Law in the Culture of Advanced Modernity," in *Common Truths: New Perspectives on Natural Law*, ed. Edward B. McLean (Wilmington, DE: ISI Books, 2000), 109.

successful communicating and negotiating include an obedience in practice to the precepts of natural law:

> A precondition for rationality in shared enquiry is mutual commitment to precepts that forbid us to endanger gratuitously each other's life, liberty, or property. And the scope of those precepts must extend to all those from whom we may at some time in our enquiry—and it is a lifelong enquiry—need to learn. So the precepts by which we will be bound, insofar as we are rational, will forbid us ever to take innocent lives, to inflict other kinds of bodily harm on the innocent, and to respect the legitimate property of others. But these are not the only types of precept whose authority must be recognized as a precondition for engagement in rational shared enquiry. If I am to engage with you in shared rational enquiry, we must both be assured that we can expect the other to speak the truth, as she or he understands it. There must be no deceptive or intentionally misleading speech.[16]

The natural law as explicitly understood is not recognized in theory by all, nor does it need to be. As Peterson points out,

> The mere fact that social order reigns to some degree does not mean that a given society has come to explicitly understand its own behavior, its own moral code.[17]

An individual and a community can observe the natural law without an explicit theory of the natural law. Likewise, a person can speak grammatically correct sentences without being able to fully articulate or explain to others the laws of grammar. Indeed, a person can speak grammatically correct sentences without ever having studied grammar, without even knowing the

---

16. Alasdair MacIntyre, "Intractable Moral Disagreements," in *Intractable Disputes about the Natural Law: Alasdair MacIntyre and Critics*, ed. Lawrence S. Cunningham (Notre Dame, IN: University of Notre Dame Press, 2009), 23.

17. Peterson, *Beyond Order*, 56.

word "grammar." The natural law is that which we cannot not know, but this knowledge may be merely practical as opposed to theoretical.

What then are the fundamental precepts of the natural law? In explaining the Ten Commandments, Peterson says,

> It is worthwhile thinking of these Commandments as a minimum set of rules for a stable society—an iterable social game.[18]

In this he echoes Aquinas, who held that the Ten Commandments are the fundamental precepts of natural law.[19] How then do the Ten Commandments relate to love? Love is, after all, what ultimately allowed Peterson to bear the suffering he describes in excruciating detail at the beginning of *Beyond Order*.

In *Beyond Order*, Peterson talks about the Ten Commandments and also the rules to love God with your whole heart and to love your neighbor as yourself, but the exact relationship between them remains opaque in his explanation. Thomas' explanation is that the Ten Commandments are themselves specifications of the command to love God with your whole heart, soul, mind, and strength and the second great command to love your neighbor as yourself. The first tablet—to have no god before God, to not use the name of the Lord in vain, and to keep holy the sabbath—all pertain to love of God. If we love God as God, as the first love of our lives, then we won't put anything else, such as money, fame, power, or pleasure, as our ultimate end in place of God. The second tablet pertains to loving our neighbor as ourselves. We do not want to be murdered, so we shouldn't murder our neighbor. We don't want to be stolen from, lied to, or cheated on, so we should avoid doing those acts to our neighbor. The law of love—loving God above all things and loving our neighbor as ourselves—is made more concrete and specific in the Ten Commandments. These commandments help us to secure our ultimate end, our ultimate goal, the final point of the journey of our lives.

18. Peterson, *Beyond Order*, 195.
19. Thomas Aquinas, *Summa theologiae* 1-2.100.1.

Aristotle held that every human action aims at an end of some kind.[20] The bricklayer, the babysitter, and the businessman do whatever they do in order to achieve some end. The proximate ends that we seek are ordered to further ends, and these ends in turn are ordered to still more remote ends. Peterson writes,

> A bricklayer may question the utility of laying his bricks, monotonously, one after another. But perhaps he is not merely laying bricks. Maybe he is building a wall. And the wall is part of a building. And the building is a cathedral. And the purpose of the cathedral is the glorification of the Highest Good. And under such circumstances, every brick laid is an act that partakes of the divine. And if what you are doing in your day-to-day activity is not enough, then you are not aiming at the construction of a proper cathedral. And that is because you are not aiming high enough.[21]

What is the ultimate aim? Aristotle and Aquinas as well thought that the ultimate end of human action was *eudaimonia*, full human flourishing, *beatitudo*, happiness. Peterson appears to disagree:

> I do not believe you should *pursue* happiness. If you do so, you will run right into the iteration problem, because "happy" is a right-now thing. If you place people in situations where they are feeling a lot of positive emotion, they get present-focused and impulsive.[22]

But might Peterson's rejection of Aristotle's view that the ultimate end of the human person is happiness rests on a disagreement about what the term "happiness" means? Is happiness really best understood as "positive emotion"? Some psychologists, like Ed Deiner,[23] define happiness as subjective

---

20. Aristotle, *Nicomachean Ethics*, 1.1, trans. Terence Irwin (Indianapolis, IN: Hackett, 2019), 1.
21. Peterson, *Beyond Order*, 135.
22. Peterson, 127.
23. Ed Diener and Robert Biswas-Diener, *Happiness: Unlocking the Mysteries of Psychological Wealth* (Malden, MA: Blackwell, 2008), 4.

positive emotion, but other psychologists, like Martin Seligman, have a more complex view. Seligman thinks of happiness as flourishing in terms of positive emotion, engagement with life, strong relationships, seeking meaning, and seeking achievement.[24] Aristotle also rejected the idea that happiness is simply positive emotion. Aristotle defined happiness as activity in accordance with virtue in a full life with friends. Positive emotion will characteristically accompany this activity for the virtuous person, as perspiration accompanies vigorous exercise. But positive emotion is a side effect of the activity of happiness, even as perspiration is a side effect of vigorous exercise. Thomas Aquinas built on Aristotle's view of happiness, but emphasized friendship with God, not just human beings, as a necessary part of the deepest kind of happiness. Following the natural law empowers us to have the deepest kind of happiness.[25]

Divine Mercy

The natural law enjoins us to be truthful and not to lie.[26] If we are to be truthful with ourselves, then we will have some painful self-realizations. As Peterson says,

> It is not just that you are lazy: it is also that you are bad—and declared so
> by your own judgment. That is a very unpleasant realization, but there is
> no hope of becoming good without it.[27]

Peterson's words affirm the reality of what Christians call sin, a missing of the mark. At the 1979 National Prayer Breakfast, Bishop Fulton Sheen made a

---

24. Martin Seligman, *Flourish: A Visionary New Understanding of Happiness and Well-Being* (New York: Simon and Schuster, 2011), ch. 1.

25. For more on this topic, see Christopher Kaczor, *The Gospel of Happiness: How Secular Psychology Points to the Wisdom of Christian Practice*, 2nd ed. (South Bend: St. Augustine's Press, 2019).

26. See Christopher Kaczor and Thomas Sherman, *Thomas Aquinas on the Cardinal Virtues: A Summa of the Summa on Justice, Courage, Temperance, and Practical Wisdom*, 2nd ed. (Washington, DC: The Catholic University of America Press, 2020) 207–215.

27. Peterson, *Beyond Order*, 359.

similar point in a room crowded with dignitaries, including the president of the United States. Thomas Reeves recounts the event:

"Mr. President," Fulton began, turning toward the chief executive and his wife, "you are a sinner." Having everyone's undivided attention, he then pointed to himself and said, "I am a sinner." He looked around the huge ballroom at the sophisticated and influential spectators, and continued, "We are all sinners, and we all need to turn to God."[28]

This realization that we are not who we could be haunts every honest person. As Peterson notes,

We are tormented equally by what we did but know we should not have done. Is this not a universal experience? Can anyone escape the pangs of conscience at four o'clock in the morning after acting immorally or destructively, or failing to act when action was necessary? **And what is the** source for that inescapable conscience? If we were the source of our own values and masters of our own houses, then we could act or fail to act as we choose and not suffer the pangs of regret, sorrow, and shame. But I have never met anyone who could manage that.[29]

How do we rectify ourselves? How can we be forgiven? Who can release us from the shame of our iniquities?

The Christian answer is Christ. Jesus is the one who delivers us from our sinfulness.[30] With his help, we can honestly face the reality of our wrongdoing in its ugliness. We can bear the enormous demand of living as if God exists. We can bear the guilt of our frequent failing to live as if God exists.

---

28. Thomas C. Reeves, *America's Bishop: The Life and Times of Fulton Sheen* (San Francisco: Encounter Books, 2001), 353.

29. Peterson, *Beyond Order*, 255.

30. Various theories of atonement examine how exactly Christ's death reconciles sinners to God. For rival models, see William Lane Craig, *Atonement and the Death of Christ: An Exegetical, Historical, and Philosophical Exploration* (Waco, TX: Baylor University Press, 2020) and Eleonore Stump, *Atonement* (New York: Oxford University Press, 2018).

The great justice of God would be crushing if it were not for the great mercy of God. Jesus is the mercy of God, the Lamb of God who takes away the sins of the world.

Everyone sins, and almost everyone at some level knows it. We create garbage simply in the course of everyday living. Catholics are blessed because they have a way of taking out this garbage. In the sacrament of Confession, Catholics name and reject the ugly garbage of sin and guilt, which are destroyed and replaced with the beautiful grace of a baby freshly baptized. As a representative of God and of the community, the ordained priest lets the penitent hear concrete and objective words of forgiveness spoken in the name of God:

> God, the Father of mercies,
> through the death and the resurrection of his Son
> has reconciled the world to himself
> and sent the Holy Spirit among us
> for the forgiveness of sins;
> through the ministry of the Church
> may God give you pardon and peace,
> and I absolve you from your sins in the name of the Father,
> and of the Son and of the Holy Spirit.[31]

If Jesus is just a symbol, if Jesus is just the ideal human being in theory, if Jesus is just a myth, then the burdens of sin and guilt are not relieved. But if Jesus was born of the Virgin Mary, suffered under Pontius Pilate, died on a Roman cross, and rose on the third day from the grave, then we have hope for our lives here below and hope for eternal life. As Pope Benedict said, "All our anxieties are ultimately fear of losing love and of the total isolation that follows from this. Thus, all our hopes are at bottom hope in the great and boundless love."[32] Without such hope, the inevitable suffering of life

---

31. *Catechism of the Catholic Church*, 1449.
32. Pope Benedict XVI, *Let's God's Light Shine Forth: The Spiritual Vision of Pope Benedict XVI*, ed. Robert Moynihan (New York: Image Books, 2005), 165.

can lead people to lose their grip on sanity. Perhaps for this reason—among others—Peterson holds that "Catholicism is as sane as people can get."[33]

The Conversion of Job

It remains to be seen where Peterson's insight will lead him moving forward. That chapter of the story is still unfolding. At the time of writing this epilogue, Peterson publicly shared that, although he has returned home after his medical ordeal, he remains in chronic pain, and that he is, in his own words, only operating at 5 percent of his previous capacity.[34] Every day remains a battle to ward off despair, to stay alive emotionally and spiritually. All is not well. Tolerable, perhaps, but not well.

In this story of prolonged suffering—the suffering of a man who has achieved great and well-deserved material success and social influence but who now finds himself in the dark—perhaps we are witnessing a modern-day Job who (we hope and pray) is only temporarily stuck in the penultimate act of the drama. After enjoying a robustly successful life, Job suddenly lost everything, including his family, including, almost, his own life. Everything fell apart. So, too, with Peterson. His wife nearly died; his daughter has had devastating long-term health issues that required treatment even at the same time as his wife—her mother—was gravely ill; and in addition to his own tortuous brush with death, there has been no shortage of ideological enemies along the way chomping at the bit to bring Peterson down, to destroy his reputation, to get him fired, to ruin him financially, and to banish him from mainstream society.

And yet Peterson, like Job, is still surviving. Indeed, parts of his life, by his own account, have dramatically improved. He has used the word

---

33. Mikhaila Peterson, "Responsibility | Mark Manson and Jordan B. Peterson on The Mikhaila Peterson Podcast #54," YouTube video, February 7, 2021, 36:22, https://youtu.be/dGDF2tTq6xw; Jordan B. Peterson, "Jonathan Pageau – Jordan B. Peterson Podcast S4 E8," YouTube video, March 1, 2021, 1:08:26, https://youtu.be/2rAqVmZwqZM.
34. "Season 4, episode 8: Jonathan Pageau," 4:03.

"miraculous" to describe the unexpected healing of his wife.[35] His daughter's health seems to be stable. The histrionic jeerers and sanctimonious would-be censors have all failed. *12 Rules for Life: An Antidote to Chaos* has sold millions of copies in numerous languages since its publication; *Beyond Order: 12 More Rules for Life* is also a great success. The last rule, rule number 12 in *Beyond Order*, says, "Be grateful in spite of your suffering." At least from what we can see from the outside—and his online presence allows a substantial view—Peterson takes his own medicine and practices what he preaches. Like Job, he has not given up, not given into the near-irresistible temptation to curse God and declare "to hell with it" because he personally continues to live in pain. He won't break the rules or, at least, won't say that the rules should be broken. That takes amazing courage and patience. Just like Job.

But it's important to remember how the story of Job concludes. Job doesn't just get his family and his possessions back. Things don't merely get better *around* him. *He* gets better too. *He* gets his own life back. Yet this release from suffering, from final tragedy, only occurs after Job realizes he had been misunderstanding the nature of God up to that point. To be sure, it wasn't that his previous understanding was false; Job always believed in *something* transcendent. Rather, it was that his understanding was *incomplete*. Prior to and through the duration of his pain, Job believed in the *idea* of God, of an idea of the transcendent, and that idea was, indeed, right enough to keep him from slipping into irredeemable despair. It was enough to keep him alive and keep him going day by day. But the problem, Job eventually realizes, is that all he had was, in fact, just an idea, just a symbol, a representation, an archetype. His idea wasn't the same as God himself. It wasn't *Yahweh*. It wasn't *the Lord*. His God was only real in the same way moonlight is real. Real enough, to be sure. But not *really* real. A reflection, not its source.

But then the conversion takes place: "I have uttered what I did not understand, things too wonderful for me, which I did not know." Job then

---

references God's words to him—"Hear, and I will speak: I will question you, and you declare to me"—and concludes: "I had heard of you by the hearing of the ear, but now my eyes see you" (Job 42:4–5).

Now my eyes see you. That is how the story ends. Job finally *sees* that the transcendent God of his intellect is a "you" and that this "you" is in *relation* with him—not only metaphysical relation but *personal* relation. Job realizes that it is therefore possible not only to talk about God but to talk *to* God ("You declare to me"). It is possible not only to think about God but to listen *to* God ("Hear, and I will speak"). It is this recognition, this awakening and free submission to the fact that the God who creates and sustains the universe is the same God who can be addressed as "you," that finally heals Job. It is that which finally puts everything back in its right place. God has not changed through the course of the story. Job has. The knower has converted into the believer, the righteous respecter of the law into the worshiper. As such, Job has abandoned his attachment to his ideas and given himself to the One who addresses him personally, who seeks him individually, and who loves him eternally. And that makes all the difference. That's what brings the story to a close. The book of Job is about suffering, yes, but it is also about the only durable antidote to suffering as well.

In the end, the difference between "acting as if God exists," which Peterson says he does, and "believing in God and acting accordingly," which Peterson says he is not ready to do, may seem inconsequential. Yet the difference between the two is as vast and relevant as the difference between reading a great love story and falling in love yourself. The right rules will certainly help you survive. But only love—both giving love and letting yourself be loved—will free you to live.

APPENDIX

Jordan Peterson and
Bishop Robert Barron: A Dialogue

This is an edited transcript of Jordan Peterson's 2019 conversation with Bishop Robert Barron on *The Jordan B. Peterson Podcast*.[1] Peterson and Bishop Barron had a second conversation on Peterson's podcast in 2021.[2]

Jordan Peterson: It's very nice to see you. I've been looking forward to our meeting for quite a long time.

Barron: Me too. Thanks for having me on the show.

Peterson: People keep writing and saying, "You have to talk to Bishop Barron," and then they come up to me and they say, "You have to talk to Bishop Barron."

Barron: I've had the same thing from the other side. Everyone's telling me to talk to you. So it must be in God's providence.

---

1. For video: Jordan B. Peterson, "Bishop Barron: Word on Fire," YouTube video, July 13, 2019, https://youtu.be/cXllaoNQmZY; for audio: "Bishop Barron: Catholicism and the Modern Age," *The Jordan B. Peterson Podcast*, June 23, 2019, https://podcasts.apple.com/us/podcast/bishop-barron-catholicism-and-the-modern-age/id1184022695?i=1000442430783.

2. For video: Jordan B. Peterson, "Christianity and the Modern World: Bishop Barron," YouTube video, April 19, 2021, https://youtu.be/BVrLqpt0APo; for audio: "Christianity and the Modern World: Bishop Barron," *The Jordan B. Peterson Podcast*, April 19, 2021, https://podcasts.apple.com/us/podcast/christianity-and-the-modern-world-bishop-barron/id1184022695?i=1000517785186.

Peterson: I suppose. At least, we can hope that that's the case. So why do people want us to talk as far as you're concerned?

Barron: I'm not entirely sure. But I would say, I think you've opened a lot of doors for people to religion in an era when the new atheists are very influential among young people—doors that legitimize at least reapproaching these great issues and questions and texts. I am doing it in a more explicit way, but you're paving the way for an awful lot of people at least to reconsider religion. So maybe they find that intriguing. And probably the fact that we're both coming out of an academic background but then trying to reach out more widely through the social media. So there's that in common.

But I just speak for myself: that's what I see in you that's been so powerful. In the wake of the new atheist critique, such a desert opens up for young people. I deal with young people all the time, and I hear the echoes of Hitchens and Dawkins and Sam Harris all the time. But it's such a finally bleak view. Religion speaks to these deepest longings of the heart, and I think you've, for a lot of people, made it again possible to at least think coherently and rationally about those things. I found that very uplifting and helpful. I think a lot of people have too, and maybe they see a point of contact there between the two of us.

Peterson: It's funny, because I've received letters from people of different faiths from all over the world—a surprising number of people. Catholics, and a lot of Orthodox Christians, a lot of Orthodox Jews, a substantial number of Muslims—far more than I would have ever suspected—Protestants and monks and Buddhists and Hindus, who are all following the lecture series I did on Genesis back in 2017. And also a tremendous number of atheists. I would say they probably outnumber the religious people, surprisingly enough, and they've said that the tack that I've taken, which is kind of a fine balancing line between the religious and the psychological . . . I guess it's had the same effect on the people that I've been talking to that it's had on me. These stories had a profound effect on me.

Barron: I've talked about you actually to the American bishops. I'm the chair of the Evangelization and Catechesis committee—the bishops concerned about how we propagate the faith today—and I've laid out for them a lot of the grim statistics (and they are grim) about especially young people leaving the Catholic Church. For every one that joins, six are leaving now. We have the highest rate of people leaving.

But then I've signaled signs of hope, and you're one of them. I said, the fact that this gentleman who is speaking about, I'd say, spiritual things, and certainly now about the Bible, in a way that is smart and compelling, especially to young people, is hopeful. Many might be leaving official religion, but the religious questions have not left their minds, and I think you're addressing that in a way that's very provocative and compelling. And it's given me a renewed courage to say, "Why can't we do the same thing?" That's our book. Let's face it: the Bible is the book that the Church has produced; it's the heart of the Church's life. But why is it that someone who is at least in a formal sense outside the Church doing a better job than we are at explicating it? And so I take it to be a sign of hope.

Peterson: It's a mystery. I feel, too, that my position outside the Church is actually critical to the success of what I'm doing. People have tried to pin me down multiple times with regards to my belief in God. I actually did a seventy-minute lecture in Australia about that question because I thought about it a lot, and I've always felt imposed upon, I would say, and boxed in when people ask me that question. But I finally figured out that I didn't really feel that I had the moral right to make a claim about belief in God. That's not a trivial thing to proclaim, because it's not merely a matter of stating in some verbal manner that I am willing to agree semantically with a set of doctrines. It means that you have to live, you have to commit to living, a certain way, and the demand of that life is so stringent and so all-consuming, and you're so unlikely to live up to it, that to make the claim that you believe—to me it smacks of a kind of . . . I understand why people do it, and this isn't a criticism of people's statement of faith.

But for me, the critical element of belief is action, and the requirements of Christianity are so incredibly demanding that I don't see how you can proclaim yourself a believer without being terrified of immediately being struck down by lightning or some such cosmic end.

Barron: There's a lot to that. There's a story that I've always loved about Origen, the great Church Father—whom Jung loved, by the way. Jung saw the Church Fathers as some of the first great psychologists, and Origen's sermons on Genesis and Exodus are like yours in many ways. I don't know if you've been reading him explicitly, but that sort of psychodynamic and spiritual reading—Origen is all over that.

But the story is about this young guy named Gregory who comes to Origen to learn the doctrine of the Christians. Origen said to him, "First, you must come and live our life, and then you'll understand our doctrine." And that young kid Gregory became St. Gregory Thaumaturgus; he becomes a great saint of the Church. But he had to get into the life first, and there's a lot to that. I think the practices of Christianity get into your body before they get into your mind.

It's also true that when you take away a lot of practices that surround certain doctrines, the doctrine fades from people's minds. When I was a kid, there was still the practice around the Blessed Sacrament with genuflection, and before you entered the pew in church, you would genuflect. In fact, they say that Catholics of my parents' generation, when they'd come into a movie theater to see a movie in the rows of seats, they would genuflect before they got into their row. That means this thing was so in their bodies. But that practice was communicating to the mind the importance of what's in front of them.

The same is true really of all the doctrines. God in some ways is a function of this manner of life. I've emphasized that actually a lot in my own work. The postmoderns, who have influenced Christianity, are very strong on that too. My take, Jordan, is that there are a hundred ways into the question of God; there's all kinds of paths, one of them being just that: ritual, the body.

The moral life is a way in. To look at the saints and to try to be a saint is a great way in.

Gerard Manley Hopkins, the great Jesuit poet, who was a convert under John Henry Newman—so he himself went through this process of discovering the faith—someone came to him and said, "I'm really wrestling with belief in God." And he said, "Give alms." In other words, he didn't provide an argument or proof; he said, *do* something. Of course, if you play the whole thing out—if God is love, and that's what God is—then performing an act of love gets you closer to God than almost anything else. So the giving of alms can lead you into that sacred space. Now, the questing mind then wants to ask all kinds of questions about it and ground it. *Fides quaerens intellectum* of Anselm—faith seeking understanding. That's where theology and philosophy will come in.

Peterson: I've been talking to my audiences practically about certain elements of Judeo-Christian fundamental beliefs. I spent I think two-and-a-half hours the first biblical lecture I did on the first sentence of Genesis, and then tried to take the opening chapters apart in great detail. But there are some very interesting propositions from a psychological and philosophical perspective in Genesis. I look at it sort of technically, in some sense, as a statement about the nature of being. What Genesis reveals to me is that there has to be a structure to encounter possibility, or that there is a structure that encounters possibility, that's built into reality itself, and that structure is God the Father. And that structure uses a process, and the process is the logos, and the logos is something like courageous, truthful communication. It's the word, but it's much more than that, and it uses that to encounter this potential and to generate order. And it seems to me that that's psychologically akin to what human beings do with their own consciousness.

The new atheist types and the materialist scientists tend to consider human beings deterministic organisms, but my understanding of neural psychology is that the only time that we are deterministic organisms is when circuits for specific tasks have been built up through lengthy practice and can be run automatically. And much of the time in our lives—and I talk to my audiences about this—what we do is we wake up in the morning, our consciousness reappears on the plane of being, and what we face in front of us is an unstructured and potential-filled chaos. Our consciousness determines the manner in which that potential transforms itself into the actuality of order into the present and the past. I think everyone understands that. We treat each other that way. We treat each other, we treat ourselves, as if we are responsible for what we bring into existence. That's part of our moral responsibility. We treat each other as if that's part of what makes us worthwhile as creatures. That's part of our value. We treat ourselves as if the nature of what we bring into being is determined by our choices between good and evil, and we treat other people the same way. You can't have a friendship with someone if you don't believe that they have that power of choice and that capacity for morality. You don't have any respect for them, and they won't interact with you, so you can't found a friendship on that, and you can't found a family. And you can't found a society without the fundamental presupposition that individuals—and this is another element, of course, of the presuppositions in Genesis—that the individual is somehow made in the image of God, if God is that which confronts potential and generates order.

And then more, because God says, too, in Genesis, that every time he constructs something that's new and orderly using the logos, he says, "And it was good." That's so fascinating to me because it's repeated so many times, because what it implies is that if the potential of being is confronted with what's good and truthful and courageous, then what emerges as a consequence is good, and I also believe that to be the case for individuals. If you confront the world in a manner that's Cain-like—bitter, incapable of making the proper sacrifices, enraged, jealous, outraged at the suffering of existence and its essential unfairness—then you become vengeful and bitter and murderous and genocidal. And that seems like no positive way forward.

Barron: That's no bargain.

Peterson: With the new atheist types, they demolish the metaphysics without really thinking it through, and they leave people with nothing. And the nothing is so empty that it just really produces pain for people. I've talked to many, many, many people, including atheists, who have been vastly relieved to find some deeper meaning in the archaic stories that our culture is predicated on.

Barron: Every day I deal with that. It's people that feel obligated intellectually to accept the new atheist conclusions, but then their whole soul is rebelling against it, and I would say for obvious reasons.

You know what's very interesting to me, Jordan, is I've got a colleague, Christopher Kaczor, who teaches at Loyola Marymount University. He's written on your stuff, and he said what Peterson is doing is what the Church Fathers would have called the tropological reading of the Scriptures. In the "four senses," you have the literal, historical interpretation; you have the allegorical, which has to do with Jesus; you have the anagogical, having to do with the journey to heaven; but the tropological they would have seen as the *moral* sense—so what it has to do about our moral lives, and I think in our categories, maybe the psychological life, etc. I think what you just proposed there is a cool tropological reading of those texts. Without denying it, I'd press on the more metaphysical stuff. Joseph Ratzinger, who became Pope Benedict XVI, did a wonderful meditation on Genesis, saying that to say "I believe in God" is to say "I believe in the primacy of Logos over and against mere matter." So, over and against a merely materialist view, what's more metaphysically primordial is Logos.

And he would stress intelligibility: the fact that God speaks the world into being means it's marked in every nook and cranny by something like intelligibility, which in turn would ground anything like the sciences. Any scientist goes out to meet a world that at least he or she assumes is intelligible. So the intelligibility of things, the rational structure within being, is coming from the Logos. But the other thing that I think is really intriguing about Genesis, that opening move, is the dethroning of all the false claims to divinity. All the things that come forth from God—the sun and moon, the animals, and so on—were all things that were worshiped in various cultures in the ancient world. So the author is saying, "No, no, no, no"—that these things are not themselves ultimate; they're not the Logos from which all things come. But then, the cool twist to me: it's not just a no. Catholics get this, because the way that text is structured is like a liturgical procession, with everything coming forth in this ordered way. At the end of the procession come human beings. So at the end of a liturgical procession is the one who will lead the praise. The point there—and this goes back to Augustine and people like that—is none of these things is God, but all these things belong in a chorus of praise of the true God led by us. And there's the human role: to give proper praise to God.

Peterson: There are critics—for example, there's a critic in Canada, a well-known environmentalist, David Suzuki—who believes that one of the sins of the Judeo-Christian perspective is that it gave human beings dominion over the world. And the German philosopher Heidegger believed that the Judeo-Christian texts had given us the right to treat the world as if it's produce.

Barron: But that's getting it exactly backward, isn't it?

Peterson: Yes.

Barron: It's this deep respect for our fellow creatures as part of the chorus of praise, and the dominion is not domination. I think it's that kind of right ordering. There's been a lot of interesting studies recently of the temple, the ancient temple, and how it was covered inside and out by symbols of the cosmos—animals and plants and planets and stars and so on—the idea being, when Israel gathered for right praise, it was the whole universe being gathered for right praise. Now, look at that in the Gothic churches; you go to Notre Dame, and it's not an anthropocentric thing. You've got the planets and stars and astrological signs and animals galore because the cathedral was the successor of the temple, the place of right praise, and it's drawing creation in. See, I think it's much more modernity that is rough on nature and rough on the animal kingdom. Thomas Aquinas is not. Go back to the premodern Christian thinkers; they're not anti-nature—on the contrary—because the biblical vision is that salvation is a cosmic reality. God's trying to save all of his creation. That's the Noah story: the ark is like a floating temple. It's a little microcosm of the right order of things led by Noah and his family.

Peterson: By a family that's properly ordered.

Barron: And what are they concerned about? The animals. They're concerned about life that God created. That's why the ark becomes a symbol of the Church. All the churches are meant to look like ships; the "nave" (*navis*, meaning ship) is the central aisle of the church. They're meant to be a little floating temple, where creation is honored and preserved.

Peterson: It's also interesting to note that in the Noah story, there's a tremendous emphasis on the idea that Noah, who's someone who, like Adam before the fall, walked with God, was capable—because he could act nobly and courageously and truthfully, and also put his family together—he was actually capable of shepherding the complex creation of being in its totality through a period of absolute chaos. When I look at the environmental challenges that we face today, because of the complexity of the nine billion of us, or the nine billion that there will be, and the necessity of making sure that everyone has adequate security and shelter and food and freedom, I see that the proper pathway forward to dealing with that is for people to put themselves together and to put their families together and their communities together, and that the natural consequence of that adoption of ultimate responsibility would be the extension of care beyond the immediate, beyond the social even. And so that everything does depend, I would say—and this is something I learned from Jung—far more than we think depends on the orderly progression and care of the soul. All of it depends on it.

When I talk to my audiences . . . this is so interesting, and I think it might be something that the Church is missing, if I could be so bold. I've talked to about 150 live audiences now about this sort of thing, independent of all my classroom lectures, and I'll tell you, I tell people, I suggest to people, the ancient idea that life is suffering and that it's tainted by malevolence, that there's no more true ideas than that in some base sense, and that that's something that everyone has to contend with and if you don't contend with it properly, then you become embittered, and you work to make things worse. And everyone understands that; everyone knows that's true. Then I suggest to them that the proper way out of that isn't the pursuit of material satisfaction or impulsive happiness or rights from the individual perspective, but the adoption of responsibility. I'll tell you, every single time I talk about that, you can hear a pin drop in the auditorium. And I think one of the things that the Church has failed to communicate properly is that you need a noble goal in life to buttress yourself against its catastrophe. Evil's a good example of that in the Abel and Cain story, because Abel devotes himself properly to God and things work out for him. Well . . .

Barron: More or less. It doesn't end very well.

Peterson: It doesn't. Good is sometimes defeated by evil. But obviously he lives a proper and admirable life. And it needs to be communicated to young people, especially young men.

Barron: The biblical key is always right praise, and I go right back to Genesis 1. When we give praise to God, drawing all creation together, then our soul becomes ordered properly, and then around us, a kingdom of right order is built up. In the Catholic Mass, we have that wonderful prayer, the Gloria. We say, "Glory to God in the highest and on earth peace to people of good will." And it's like a formula: if I give glory to God in the highest, then there will be peace around me.

Peterson: That's like a condensation of the Sermon on the Mount. That's exactly what that sermon seems to me, and I also believe it to be psychologically true: that it's necessary for you to aim at the highest value that you can conceive of, and that has to have something to do with the amelioration of suffering and the constraint of malevolence.

Barron: It'll express itself that way naturally.

Peterson: It has to have something to do with that. At least as a negative. And then, once you concentrate on that, focus on that, and decide that that's your primary aim, then things do start to order themselves around you because everything that you see and do directs itself toward that aim.

Barron: But that's the strangely and uniquely Christian thing. We say the God that we're worshiping is the God revealed in the Old Testament but then finally revealed in Jesus Christ. As I'm looking over my computer screen right now, I'm looking at the crucifix of Jesus. My praise is directed to a God who has entered radically into suffering—not just physical suffering but the whole brokenness of the world, of stupidity and cruelty and injustice and hatred. That's where God has gone. So the God that I worship is the God who himself is dedicated to the amelioration of suffering or of healing the suffering of the world.

But that's the way it's going to express itself in a fallen, conflictual world. Right praise will end up looking like love for those who suffer. That's to me the master theme of the whole Bible. Israel always goes wrong without exception when its praise goes wrong. It starts praising the wrong things.

Peterson: That's what happens in Exodus when Moses leads the Israelites through the desert. They're in the same position we're in in the modern world, where we've escaped a tyranny of sorts, or we believe we have, and entered into this domain of untraveled freedom, and there's nothing but false idols calling to us from every direction. That's the diversity idea as far as

I'm concerned, because unity is certainly as profound a moral necessity as diversity. There should be diversity within unity.

Barron: I fight it all the time—in the Church, too, because we bought into that ideology. It's the oldest problem in philosophy, the one and the many. But all we do today is completely valorize the many; we never see its shadow side. We denigrate the one, and never see its positive side. The one is extraordinarily important.

Peterson: That's part of the death of God. It's the death of that overarching unity. It's the same thing that drives constant thoughtless criticisms of hierarchy, even though all the biological evidence suggests you can't even organize your perception without using an ethical hierarchy, because you have to select from all the things that you can choose to look at—those things that you value high enough to attend to.

Barron: And that's our point about worship, isn't it? What's of highest value to you? Everything else will follow from that.

Paul Tillich, the great Protestant theologian, said that all you need to know about a person you can find out by asking one question: What does he worship? And everyone of course does; Sam Harris worships something. "Worth-ship"—what's of highest worth to you? Then your life will be organized accordingly. The biblical idea, it seems to me, is if it's other than God, you will *dis*integrate on the inside, and the society around you will disintegrate.

Peterson: That's where the idea of the logos has been so helpful to me, partly as a consequence of reading Jung. If the logos is that element of being that's allied in some sense with consciousness, that does in fact confront potential, and that does cast it into reality as a consequence of ethical choices, then I can't see how it can be otherwise than that has to be regarded as the ultimate value, because it's the thing that continually creates the world anew. And we know perfectly well that you can take the opposite tack. Let's say I don't worship courage and truth in the face of the potential of being, and that I worship instead cowardice and deceit and vengefulness. Well, we know where that goes. We had the entire twentieth century as a—

Barron: It's the template for that whole thing.

Peterson: And the template from every perspective. It's obvious; it's obvious beyond a shadow of arguable doubt that human beings as individuals are capable of generating something around them that is so akin to hell, even metaphysically speaking, that you have to be picayune to quibble about the difference. And I do think there's something metaphysical about it. These things that we see on Earth seem to me to be reflected continually at deeper and deeper levels of reality. I don't tend to talk about specifically religious issues, because I think that would, in some sense, compromise the approach that I'm attempting to take, which is a conciliatory approach in some sense between those who are possessed by the scientific viewpoint but curious about the religious viewpoint. But if you abandon those initial presuppositions—the sovereignty of the individual, the necessity for courage in the face of being, the moral imperative to struggle uphill with your cross towards the city of God—people understand these things if they're explained carefully, and they know in their souls that they're true.

Barron: And they're all over the culture. That's been a presupposition of mine doing this work: I tend not to begin with direct instruction or moral finger-wagging, but I tend to begin with something going on in the culture. And you've talked about this: the hero myth is in practically every movie you watch.

But the Christian themes are every place, one of the most remarkable to me being Clint Eastwood's *Gran Torino*. It is the best exemplification in fiction, I think, of what the Church Fathers meant by the meaning of Jesus' cross—in other words, a move of self-sacrificing love that exposes evil and liberates those who are under the tyranny of evil. That's how they read the cross in a very clever way—expressed in more mythic language—but the ideas are very powerful, and they're beautifully exemplified in that movie. The move that Eastwood's character makes at the end—and of course, as he dies, he's in the figure of the crucified Jesus, lest we miss the point.

Peterson: It's so interesting, too, because I actually made a video where I used a picture of Christ delivering the Sermon on the Mount, I think, and I put Clint Eastwood's face. I superimposed it on top of his. And it was for exactly that reason, the reason that's exemplified in *Gran Torino*. Because Eastwood in that movie is a very harsh character, very judgmental. He's like the Christ that comes back in Revelation. He's very, very, very judgmental, and he cuts no one a break—except that he actually does. He does separate the wheat from the chaff, and he even, interestingly, in that movie, ends up being more akin to the foreigners who he hypothetically hates. "Who's the Good Samaritan?" It's the same idea as the Good Samaritan. He becomes more family to these people that he hypothetically hates than to his own children because he regards them as ungrateful and unworthy, whereas these new immigrants are striving to be good people. It's a very interesting movie.

Barron: It is, and it's a good example of a principle one of my professors years ago said: the once-integrated Christian vision, after the Reformation and the Enlightenment, blew up, and the pieces flew every place. And they're twisted and they're charred, and they've landed here and there. So as you go through the cultural landscape, you see them all over the place. There's a bit of eschatology, or there's Christology, or there's the Trinity, and so on. But they're usually in distorted form. That's a good example of there's the Christus Victor theory, to give it its proper name: that Christ is the victor over sin and death; he's conquered the dark powers and liberated us in the process. There it is, but it's in somewhat distorted form, of course. But that's been the game I've played a lot is to try to find these bits and pieces.

Peterson: It happens everywhere. It's so common. It isn't merely common; it's universal. This is, of course, one of the reasons that I became so deeply interested in archetypes is that, if the story doesn't have an archetypal foundation, then it's not a story. Something makes something a story; it's not just a random collection of statements or images. It has an archetypal structure. And I think what's happened in the modern world, at least partly, is this fractionation that you've described, but also something that a student once made me think deeply through. She came up and asked me after class: If these archetypal stories are the fundamental element of psychobiological reality, then why not just tell the archetypal story over and over again? I thought, first of all, to some degree, that is what cultures did for a long time. They just repeated the archetypal story. But in our modern culture, what literature seems to do is to take the archetypal story and to bring it closer to the individual. It's like it's brought closer to Earth, almost like the Renaissance paintings brought the divine figures closer to Earth, closer to the actual individual, say, than the Baroque paintings did. So you have this meeting place of the divine, the archetype, and the personal that constitutes something like popular culture. There's some utility in that, because it reopens a doorway to the presence of what's missing that's been closed by whatever has happened to the Church over the last 150 to 200 years, and the accelerating degeneration of the Church over the last 150 to 200 years.

So I see it as a good thing, although it isn't obvious that people understand that it's happening. I explain movies like *The Lion King* and *Sleeping Beauty* and so on to my audiences, and they don't consciously see the Christian symbolism. Or the Christian symbolism in works like *Harry Potter*, which is unbelievably deep symbolic structure. She did that so beautifully.

Barron: There is this remake of *True Grit*, when the Coen brothers did it, and they beautifully brought out these religious themes that were not in the John Wayne version that I saw as a kid. Or even there was a remake Kenneth Branagh did of *Cinderella*. And you might say it's a charming, sentimental story, but it's a deeply Christological telling, and he got all that and brought that out. So those are there for sure within the Western framework.

Peterson: I've been accused—although I've stopped apologizing for it, and I should have stopped long ago—of fundamentally speaking to young men. Most people on YouTube are men, so there's a baseline problem. But it seems to me that partly what I'm suggesting to young men is that there really is an ennobling heroism about the fundamental Christian vision, which is to accept with gratitude your privileges and your limitations. The privileges, those are talents; you have a responsibility to make the most of them. That's the price you pay for the talents. The obstacles: you're a limited being and you pay a price for being and the price is that limitation, and so you have to be grateful in some strange sense for your limitations, maybe the same way that you're grateful for the idiosyncrasies and peculiarities of the people that you love. Then, that your task—it's an extraordinarily difficult task, and there's no more challenging task—is to accept all that with gratitude and with goodwill toward being and to attempt to work toward making things better than they are, or at least not worse. People understand that.

Barron: Let me press something here. Because I think all that's true from the sort of psychological and human side: the hero's journey and our call to move toward a transcendent moral good, etc., to give ourselves for the sake of the other. That's all there within the Christian and the biblical framework. But what I think is really interesting—where the fireworks really start—is that God has gone on a hero's journey. It's not just the story of this human being Jesus going heroically to his cross, etc., but that, strangely, it's God going heroically to that place. It's God going into dysfunction. And whatever heroism we can summon is predicated upon this primordial grace that was given to us.

I'm a Catholic; Catholics like faith and reason. So we like to operate on both sides of that divide. So, Thomas Aquinas constructing cosmological arguments—good. Those are fine. But that's from our side of the equation. We're kind of moving our way toward God. But the fireworks start when God moves toward us. God acts, and grace is operative, this thing that I can't manipulate, I can't control, it comes as a gift. And so at the cross of Jesus, it is Clint Eastwood. There's a human being imitating this great move, and that's indeed what we're called to: to become other Christs. But he's also, if you want to press it, God. That's what God does. God enters into our weird, dysfunctional, off-kilter world and suppresses evil, awakens our freedom. And that's when it really gets interesting.

Peterson: It seems to me that this has to do with this theme I've also popularized about rescuing your dead father from the underworld. If you take on a heavy burden of responsibility, then that changes you; it calls forth from you things that would never be otherwise called forth, partly because you encounter new things and learn, but also because the psychophysiological demands of the confrontation—and we know this biologically—turn on new parts of you that are coded genetically. There's an immense potential that lurks inside of human beings, and it's a potential of unlimited scope in some sense. I think that that's alluded to in the idea that there's a relationship between logos, Christ, and God and man, and that the way that you become closer to God in the literal sense is by adopting that burden because that transforms you into what it is that you could be.

The other thing you said that was really interesting, you talked about the fragmentation of Christianity. In the old Egyptian story, Osiris is overthrown by Seth, who's the precursor of Satan, etymologically and conceptually. Osiris is willfully blind, and Seth is his evil brother, and Seth waits for the opportune moment and he chops Osiris up into pieces, and he distributes him all over the kingdom. So Osiris can't pull himself back together. He's still there in nascent form because there's no destroying something that's divine—not permanently—but you can make it very difficult for it to get its act together for some period of time. That fragmentation has occurred in our culture. The death of God—I think Nietzsche is wrong about that.

I think it's the dismemberment of God, not the death. Something that's dis-membered can be re-membered, and what we need to do is to remember. And we do remember in our literature and our art and our popular culture. That's all a form of remembering. But we also remember when we act in a way that works in accordance with our conscience, and that sets our soul into a configuration of peace.

It's been fascinating. I've had hundreds—mostly young men, I would say—come and talk to me after my lectures. And many of them had been in very, very dark places—addicted, alcoholic, suicidal, chronic pornography users incapable of settling into a committed relationship, vengeful, nihilistic, cynical, and also possessed by a kind of inertia that made them immobile during the most vital part of their youth. And they told me, "I decided I was going to develop a vision for my life. I was going to imagine what things could be, and then I was going to try to tell the truth, and I was going to try to act responsibly, and not in a praying-in-public manner but in a manner that began with cleaning up my room, a fairly humble act." And then comes the kicker, and this is one of the things that's kept me going through this entire 150-city tour. They all say, "And my life is way better. I'm healthy, my job is going well, I've had three promotions. I'm making twice as much money. I've spoken to my father—I haven't talked to him for ten years. I'm putting my family together." Good things are just happening left, right, and center. I heard amazing stories.

Barron: You're in touch with the deepest rhythms of reality. It's an ethical move, but it's a metaphysical move. You mentioned the Sermon on the Mount of the Lord. That's how I look at it: it's not just giving moving ethical recommendations. It's trying to get us aligned to the fundamental nonviolence of things, the fundamental move of God as he gives rise to the world. And so, of course your life comes together. Again, right praise gets you on line and knits you back together. That theme to me is really strong in the spiritual tradition: the knitting back together of the splintered self.

Peterson: It's the coming together of things.

Barron: As a psychotherapist, you deal all the time with this. But in the Scriptures—you mentioned Satan, *ho Satanas*, is the accuser, and there's a lot to that—but the other great word for the dark power is the *diabolos*, the scatterer, the one that divides and separates. The demon is always speaking in the plural in the New Testament, and Jesus is bringing the possessed back to themselves, back to the center. But that's all of us sinners; we're all over the place. Our mind and will and passions and sexuality and body—they're all going different directions.

Peterson: It's very disorienting for people. It's very confusing and anxiety-provoking to be going in all those directions at the same time.

Barron: Yes. "What do you want of us, Jesus of Nazareth? Have you come to destroy us?"[1] The answer is, "Yes, I have come to destroy this disparate reality and knit you back together."

Go back to Nietzsche for a second, because I want to ask you about that. My conviction is that atheists both old and new—so Hitchens and Dawkins and Sam Harris today, but then go back to Feuerbach, Nietzsche, and company—they're rebelling quite properly against a false god, what I would characterize as a false god: the god who is posing a threat to our freedom, the God who broods over us in this moralizing and dehumanizing way, the God who I would say is a supreme being among other beings—all of that. I applaud them; the atheists, old and new, are rebelling against that. But it's partially because—and I think Jung saw this in his own father, who was a Calvinist minister—we got so bad at proclaiming the true God, who is not brooding over our freedom in this sort of moralizing and oppressive way, who's not competing with our flourishing. "The glory of God is a human being fully alive," says

---

1. Mark 1:24.

Irenaeus. That's the biblical idea. Or the burning bush—the Fathers loved that—which is the bush that's on fire but not consumed. That's the way the true God relates to creation: he makes it beautiful and radiant but doesn't burn it up.

Whereas, in so many of the Greek and Roman myths, when the gods break in, things have to give way or they're incinerated or they're destroyed. But the Bible presents this very unique and humanizing view of God, which culminates in the Incarnation: God becomes one of us. That's why it's so beautiful to me in those seemingly abstract formulas about the two natures that come together in Jesus without mixing, mingling, and confusion. You might say that that's a lot of these Greek abstractions. But no, that's very powerful: that God and humanity can meet in such a way that humanity is not overwhelmed and destroyed. That's what the atheists, quite rightly, old and new, are objecting to: precisely that false understanding of God.

Peterson: It's a very disturbing analogy, but I've always thought of Nietzsche playing the same role as maggots do when they're cleaning out a wound. He's a very sophisticated thinker, and to think of Nietzsche simply as an atheist is a terrible mistake. He certainly had plenty of good things to say about Catholicism, about the fact that Catholicism was an anti-diabolical movement that united Europe under the rubric of a single mode of thought and disciplined the European mind. And he also had wonderful things to say about Christ as a figure. Nietzsche believed that the only true Christian was Christ, and his criticism was essentially saved for the dogmatic structure of the Church. Now, I actually have more sympathy for Dostoyevsky, who I think thought more deeply about this than Nietzsche, which is quite a frightening thing to say because Nietzsche is such a deep thinker.

But in "The Grand Inquisitor," when Christ comes back to earth and is then arrested by the Grand Inquisitor of Seville during the Spanish Inquisition, the Grand Inquisitor takes Christ into the cell and tells him why it's necessary for him to be put to death again. He says the Church has worked diligently to humanize the impossible load that you've placed on people and to make it bearable for the common man. And the last thing we need is someone as perfect as you—and terrifying as a consequence as a judge, because something that perfect is a judge—coming back to mess up all our work. That's a sympathetic portrayal of Catholicism, I would say, or maybe Orthodox Christianity as well; that it had that merciful element that the demand for perfection was antithetical to. But then of course Dostoyevsky has the brilliance to say that when the Grand Inquisitor leaves, hypothetically having sentenced Christ to death, he leaves the door open. And I've often thought that that's so true of Catholicism and Orthodox Christianity—Protestantism as well—is that for all their faults, and for all the faults that people like Nietzsche, and Hitchens, and Dawkins, etc. lay at the feet of these traditions, they at least did preserve the tradition and leave the door open. That's not an easy thing to do over the course of centuries. I think the institutions deserve a certain amount of sympathy, even though I'm very concerned that they're degenerating and disintegrating in a manner that doesn't look easily forestallable.

Barron: Let me ask you a quick question about *The Brothers Karamazov*, because twice in my life, I tried to read it, and I think I just got bogged down with the Russian names. So I failed both times—I got a little further the second time. But then just about six months ago, I got an audio of it—because I'm in the car all the time in California, going back and forth—and I'm just about finished with it. I love it. It finally just sang to me as this guy read.

Peterson: It's amazing how powerful it is on audio.

Barron: It's wonderful. How do you read, first of all, the silence of Christ in the presence of the Inquisitor, but then secondly, the kiss on the lips at the end? He sits in silence as this great accusation is read, but then kisses him on the lips at the end.

Peterson: I think he accepts the accusation. One of the things Jung said about Christ in the Gospels, which I thought was indescribably brilliant, was that Christ—not entirely—is presented as a figure of mercy. And Jung was wise enough to know, and he used religious sources for this idea, that God rules with two hands: with mercy and with justice. Because if it's just mercy, then all is always forgiven and you have no responsibility, and you're an eternal infant. But if it's all justice, then look out, because every single transgression you commit, you'll be held to account for in some infinite manner. And people are so fallible. You kind of see that happening on Twitter now. If you make a mistake of any sort at any point in your life, you're roasted over the open coals for it. No one can stand that because everyone makes mistakes. So there has to be this balance between mercy and justice. And Jung regarded Christ's return in Revelation as psychologically necessary, because any figure of perfection has this element of the judge, because any ideal is a judge.

Barron: You can't bracket that. The master category is love. That's not to be sentimental about it; love means to will the good of the other. So that always has a judgmental dimension to it.

Peterson: Of course it does. Because if you have a child, or a friend, or yourself . . . and I felt this when I was practicing as a psychotherapist. Rogers said you had to have unconditional love for your client. I thought, no; I have unconditional positive regard for the part of my client that's striving toward the light, and I am a co-enemy with that part against the part that's trying to drag that person down.

Barron: An entire generation of Catholic priests was formed under the Rogerian assumption, because that's what my generation got. Now, I learned things from Rogers. It works in a way—when I was doing pastoral ministry and counseling early on as a young priest—that whole idea of just kind of mirroring back to someone what they're saying. I get it. But I agree with you:

there's a severe danger in that. If that's all we're doing with people, we're not moving them in the manner of a spiritual teacher.

I had a student years ago who said to me, "What we're missing from the Church is Yoda on our shoulders." He meant Yoda on the shoulders of Luke Skywalker, instructing him and pressing him and telling him what he's doing wrong and how to get going. We were all Rogerians; we just were unconditionally positively regarding everybody.

Peterson: It's a great compliment. The other thing that's made me popular among young people . . . and this is so perverse. I have a hard time believing any of it really. The first thing that I have a hard time believing is that I can attract audiences of five thousand people and tell them that the problem with their lives is that they're not bearing nearly enough responsibility, and that's where they're going to find the meaning that sustains them. It's a pretty rough message. And the second thing is, especially with young people, the message has been for fifty years—and this is part of the humanists from the 1960s—is "You're okay the way you are." I think there isn't anything more damning that you can tell a young person than "You're okay the way you are"—especially if they're suffering and nihilistic.

Barron: They're saying, "Get me out of who I am. I want to get out of this state."

Peterson: That's right. They want to crawl right out of their skin. And so you tell them instead, "No, look: you don't know anything. You're barely beginning. You're suffering, in a sense, because you are steeped in sin to an almost unimaginable degree. And I'm saying that compassionately, not judgmentally. If you want to put your life together, you have to start small, and you have to be careful and awake. If you do it carefully, then you can eliminate these flaws in your character that no one should be celebrating." People light up when you tell them that. It's so strange.

Barron: It was a real pastoral failure on the part of the Church as I was coming of age, because we were reacting against maybe a hyper-stress on sin—my parents' generation probably got that—especially sexual sin. So I understand that there was a hyper-reaction. But that is exactly the problem: you ended up with a generation of Catholics that said, "God is love. I'm okay. Everything will be fine." Then there's no energy, there's no directionality, there's no sense of purpose, there's no sense of spiritual struggle.

Peterson: There's no evil. That's a real problem when you're dealing with situations like Nazi Germany.

Barron: Right. That was a huge pastoral failure. One problem was intellectual as I was coming of age—we became very deeply anti-intellectual—and this problem of a hyper-Rogerianization of our pastoral practice.

Peterson: I liked Rogers a lot, because one of the things Rogers really taught me to do was to listen. His advice about listening and then restating to people what you heard so that they agree with you—that's unbelievably powerful, because it does force you to listen. But Rogers was a seminarian, and he did dispense with the idea of evil and the devil, fundamentally. He fell into the trap of Rousseau, where the idea was that people were basically good. That's just such a devaluation of people to say that they're basically good, because it's clearly the case that people have an unbelievable capacity for malevolence. And to me that's heartening.

Again, I can talk to my audiences, and I can say, "Look, you guys just sit on the edge of your bed and you think about all the things that you're doing wrong, that you know that you're doing wrong, and the way that you're leading yourself and other people astray. Those things will come to your mind momentarily. And imagine briefly where that would take you if you allowed your imagination to take you to where it could in its depths." And everyone nods their head, because they bloody well know. And I say, "Imagine just for a moment that if you have that capacity for absolute mayhem and malevolence, that the opposite is also true. Because if there is that darkness and that evil, then obviously the opposite also exists." Then it's also possible to make a case to people that they can believe that good has the capability of triumphing over evil. But you don't do that by minimizing evil; you do it by maximizing evil.

Barron: I would say part of spiritual direction is helping people see what they're really capable of, and I mean that in the negative sense: helping people to see that they're really capable of some really wicked business. If they're hiding from that all the time, they're suppressing it all the time, that's not the thing to do. Because—from a religious standpoint, now—you want to say, Christ goes all the way down. Now, that's the descent into hell theme, but that happens in us. He goes all the way down in me to the bottom of my dysfunction. And people like Dostoyevsky are really good at showing that dimension of life.

But if we don't do that spiritually, then we're not understanding the cross; we're not understanding redemption, salvation—that we're healed by this downward journey of the Son of God, but he goes with us. There's Dante now; there's the journey downward through all the levels of our dysfunction until you find—and I think he's dead right about that—some originating dysfunction: the Satan whose wings beat the air and create the atmosphere of hell. There's something in me that's generating all the different levels of dysfunction. But until I find that, I'm not going to solve it. I've got to go all the way down.

Peterson: The *Inferno* is right. Just like there's a hierarchy of good, there's a hierarchy of evil. Dante places the betrayers at the bottom with Satan. And I think that's true, because one of the fundamental necessities of positive interpersonal existence—even with yourself, let alone other people—is trust, essential trust. And it's a form of courage. Another thing I talk to my audiences about is trust, because we tend in our society to worship naïve trust by making the claim that people are basically good. The problem with that—and this is what entices so many young people into that nihilistic atheism—is that they're taught this idea, and then they're betrayed very badly by themselves or by some other person. That's the death of innocence. Then they go from naïveté to cynicism, and cynicism is actually an improvement over naïveté. But it's not the end. And they don't know that because the next step is to trust as a consequence of courage, and to say: I'm going to extend my hand once again to myself or to my friend or to my family member, despite the fact that I've already been betrayed and hurt, because by extending that hand again, I allow the person the possibility of redemption, and I open up a space for us to rekindle a productive relationship. But that's predicated on courage and not naïveté. It's like stretching out a hand to a dog that's frightened, barking, and looking like it's going to bite. It's still the best way, if you're careful, to establish peace with that animal. The problem with the betrayers is that they take trust, which is the most fundamental necessity for interpersonal relationships, and then they violate the very principle of trust, and it undermines everything.

Barron: And that's why they're at the bottom of hell. That's why Cassius and Brutus and Judas are there.

It reminds me of that story of Francis and the Wolf of Gubbio. It's like a dream, that story—Francis reaching out to the animal that's been threatening the town and frightening everybody—but Francis has the trust to reach out to the animal and then he tames it, and then makes a deal: if you feed the animal, then he won't harm you, and so on. But doesn't Jung say that in a lot of dreams animals function that way—dimensions of ourselves that we're avoiding?

Peterson: That's a dream, for sure. Because what it means is that there's a part of you that's ravenous and malevolent and—

Barron: Not being fed properly.

Peterson: Right. And that's often because you're not attending to it. You're putting it in a blind corner. And it's acting out because it demands recognition. People do this with the power that gives them integrity.

I've had clients, and I would say they were more often female than male, who had this particular problem, but who had a very acute and judgmental intelligence. Very, very bright people. But they were also unbelievably agreeable. Their intelligence would report to them something that was not positive about someone. It would see around the corner; it would see into a hidden motivation and reveal a negative truth. And the person temperamentally was so shocked by the revelation that instead of regarding it as a genuine insight, they felt that there was something wrong with them for thinking that way. That's the same thing as keeping that ravenous wolf unfed. The particular client I'm thinking about, I spent hours talking to her about what she thought about people, because she was a very pleasant person and it caused her a lot of trouble. She was far too much mercy and not nearly enough justice. Her insights into the malevolent motivations of people were unbelievably accurate and deep, but she was almost completely incapable of allowing that to be real.

Barron: That reminds me of—I mentioned it earlier—the Coen brothers' remake of *True Grit*. Remember the young girl in that who's just seized by justice, she wants to get revenge because her father was killed. People are dying around her, corpses are piling up, because she's just going to get what she wants. Then of course, she's bit by the snake, which has a certain archetypal overtone, and she loses her arm. But she's carried, after the snake bite, in the two arms of Rooster Cogburn, who's a law man, he's a man of justice, but you find out that he's also a man of mercy. He's a man of deep human connection. The story is prefaced by the line: "There's only one thing in the world that's truly free, and that's the grace of God." The grace of God is not just mercy and not just justice. It's the two arms of it. She ends up all justice—the one arm's missing—but Rooster's got the two arms, able to carry her. But I think that's what we've been missing a lot in the Church is the two arms. We've become just too much of a mercy Church, in a way.

Peterson: That's what I think. I don't think that you guys ask enough of your people. You're not giving them hell.

Barron: I think there's something right about that, and that's the Yoda on your shoulders: someone who's kind of pushing me and telling me and teaching me and bringing me on that downward journey. The Virgil move: that you're going to accompany this person all the way down. Now, here's why Pope Francis is really good: he speaks of accompaniment, and the Church is a field hospital, he says, for people deeply wounded. That's really right. And we've got to accompany people—though all the way down. My generation got a very superficial "Everything's okay. God is love. And you'll be fine." But that led to a lot of drift. When my generation came of age, and we got hit by life, I can testify there's a lot of my classmates that left religion in a heartbeat. We got a very superficial, childish, one-sided approach, but then life hits all of us inevitably, and religion had nothing for them.

Peterson: And that's exactly when it's necessary. Love is a terrible thing. It's demanding. If you love your children, you don't let them get away with anything. You call them on their transgressions.

I remember this situation with my son when he was about four or five. I have a really good relationship with my son. I've always assumed that he had the capability to make intelligent judgments and expected him to do so from a very early age. When he was four, he was talking to me and I thought he was lying to me. And I didn't know, because I couldn't tell, but that internal daemon was saying, no, there's something that's not right here. And I wasn't going to let him get away with it because I couldn't let him learn that it was acceptable to do that, or that I would put up with it. So I told him in this weird thing—it's kind of like Pharaoh, or it's kind of like God hardening Pharaoh's heart—I said, here's the deal. I think you're lying to me, and we can't have that. But if you're not, I want you to put up a tremendous fight here to defend yourself. Because if you're being honest, then I want to know that. But I'm not going to back off, because I don't believe that what you're saying is true. So I went after him for a good long while, and it did turn out that he was telling me something that wasn't true, which hardly came as a relief. Children do that, and it wasn't a surprise to me. But if you really love someone, you can't tolerate when they're less than they could be. It hurts.

So when someone comes into the Church and it's all forgiveness, there's no care there. It's like: What the hell are you doing? Look at you. You're addicted. You're hooked on pornography. You cheat on your wife. You're doing a terrible job at work. You don't take care of yourself. What the hell's wrong with you? Where's the real you? Anyone who is subject to that . . . as long as it's done with care, and not "I'm better than you," which is a whole different thing. It's like: You're nothing like you should be.

Barron: And if you don't do that, you're not willing the good of the other. In fact, you're trying to move into an easy space: if I'm nice to this person, he'll be nice to me, and we'll all be happy. But that's not love; that's just sentimentality.

Peterson: It's a no-conflict conversation.

Barron: It reminds me of the beginning of the *Inferno* when Dante sees the hill with light on it and says, "There it is; that's where I need to go. I know I'm lost, I'm in the wood, but that's where I need to go." And off he goes. But then he's blocked by the three animals: the wolf, the leopard, and the lion. There's no easy route; that's the point. There's no easy route to that hill. You've got to go down, and all the way down. We probably did tell our people that it was too easy a route. "Everything's okay. You're okay. God is love."

Peterson: "God is love, and love is nice."

Barron: Love is "harsh and dreadful."

Peterson: That's the thing. Love *is* harsh and dreadful.

Barron: And they'll find out soon enough that the road is blocked; everyone does. But then, what's the way forward? There should be spiritual masters in place that know exactly what to do—the Virgil move: "I know what we've got to do here. We've got to do a searching moral inventory and go all the way down."

Peterson: All the way down. That's the descent before the ascent. That's a classical fall-of-man story. It's the story of Exodus. It's part of the reason that people aren't enlightened. If you're going to go up, every up is predicated by a down of equivalent magnitude. If you're going to improve, you're going to discover that you're wrong about something first, and then to be wrong about something means you're going to fragment, and it's going to be painful to recognize the fact of that error, to recognize the consequences of that error across your life, to have to reformulate yourself so that that error is no longer acting out as part of your personality in your life. It's an unbelievable descent.

This is part of the reason why, for all the respect I have for Joseph Campbell, Campbell says, "Follow your bliss." And that is certainly not something that Jung said, because Jung said you search out what you're most terrified of and what you're most disgusted by and the place you least want to go, where you have to bow the lowest, and that's the place where salvation might be found. I believe that's true, and I believe it's terrifying. The pathway to redemption is through recognition of error, not through bliss. That was where Campbell got enamored of a kind of mindless Buddhism.

Barron: The only way up is down, and that's in all the spiritual teachers. Or go back to Origen—you mentioned Exodus—where he says that the Egyptians and the Israelites symbolize that the best of us is often enslaved to the worst of us. The Egyptians, the slave masters, represent the worst instincts in us, and the most twisted and dysfunctional aspects of us. And the Israelites symbolized, he felt, our creativity, our intelligence, our courage, our friendship, all these good things.

Peterson: Our willingness to move forward.

Barron: The best of us is enslaved to the worst of us. So you've got to come to terms with who are the Egyptians in you. And they're making you do two things, he says. They're making you build fortified cities for them—so we take the best of ourselves to build fortifications around the worst of ourselves to protect them—and they build monuments: "Hey, look at me." How much of life, he says, is spent doing those two dysfunctional things: defending the worst of ourselves, and then building monuments to the worst of ourselves? When, in fact, we've got to get free of that and get to the promised land. But he was the original master of all that psychodynamic reading of these texts.

Peterson: But it's also surprising that so few people know what a multiplicity of readings the Bible has actually withstood.

Barron: Because we get hung up on this goofy fundamentalism, which is a twentieth-century phenomenon—the Scopes trial and all of that. We in America especially, but in the West more generally, we got hung up on it. You read Augustine, who is deeply indebted to Origen, you've got these very creative interpretive strategies in place—around Genesis, for example. It's not literalism by any means. We're talking Origen; we're talking the third century. Irenaeus, second century. Augustine, fourth century. These are really early figures, and they're not hung up on literalism.

Peterson: And these were mystical thinkers. They weren't scientists.

Barron: Right. Yes, we need to recover that, even as Christians, our own biblical interpretive tradition.

Peterson: So what are you hoping for in the coming year for you and for what you're doing? What would you like to see happen as a consequence of what you're doing? And what do you think you are doing? I mean you're on this public—I wouldn't call it a crusade—but you're engaging with the public in this new way, and it seems to be quite successful. What do you think it is that you're doing right, and what would you like to see happen as a consequence of that?

Barron: I think what I'm doing right is beginning with the *semina verbi*—it's the Church Fathers' idea—the "seeds of the Word." The seeds of the Word are everywhere; that's the bits of the fragmented Catholicism that are found in the culture. So I tend to begin with the culture and lead from there. I think that is more winsome. So I tend not to begin with a lot of preaching or a moralizing approach. I begin with a cultural approach. I think that's been more appealing.

My ultimate goal is to bring people to faith in Christ in the Catholic Church. That's my ultimate goal. I'm an evangelizer. But I'm using certain methods to try to draw people to that point, realizing that there's an awful lot of obstacles in the way. I'm trying to kick open some doors. Part of it is to help people with their intellectual blocks. There are so many, especially younger people, that are just stuck, because certain intellectual objections have occurred to them, and they've heard them from their university professors or whatever. To clear up some of that, to knock over some of those obstacles, that's part of what I'm trying to do. But then to open up—and I think that's what you're doing too—the richness of this spiritual tradition, because it's not just an intellectual feast; it saves your soul. That's what I want to do. Your fellow Canadian Charles Taylor, the great Catholic philosopher, talks about the buffered self, the self that's caught in this little space, and there's no sense of a link to the transcendent. I'm trying to knock holes in the buffered self and let in some light from a higher dimension of reality. So ultimately to bring people to salvation, I would say, is what I want to do. But I also want to keep knocking holes in the buffered self.

I was in Rome in October—we had this month-long synod with the pope on young people, and I was elected to go to that synod. It was interesting. What's our strategy for reaching young people? I said, I think a miracle of providence right now is we have this massive problem of young people leaving, but we have this new tool of the social media, which we didn't have. Ten years ago, we couldn't do this. Yet now we can reach out to young people, into their space. Because as Catholics, we tend to say, "What programs can we develop? What lecture series can we develop?" People aren't coming to our institutions for all kinds of reasons. But we can sort of move into their space with the social media. So that's kind of how I see what I'm up to and trying to do.

Peterson: It would be nice to see if something could be done with all those beautiful cathedrals.

Barron: I wrote about them years ago. I studied in Paris, and I used to give tours at Notre Dame. I was a doctoral student—I was a priest, but a doctoral student. And we were told by the tour guides, "Now, don't talk about religion." We were just meant to talk about how tall the building was, and when it was built. But I used it to sermonize, really, to talk about the Christian faith. I've written a little book on the spirituality of the cathedrals: *Heaven in Stone and Glass*.

Peterson: I'd like to read that. Is there a decent bibliography in that book? Because I'm really interested in cathedral architecture.

Barron: No, and I am too. I wrote this years ago. It's a little book of kind of spiritual meditation, so it wouldn't be with an academic apparatus. But I read a lot of those books at the time and loved the cathedrals too. Talk about moving into a dream space; archetypal realities are all over the place. Chartres is my favorite place in the world, maybe. My favorite covered space in the world is Chartres Cathedral.

Peterson: Why that cathedral?

Barron: I don't think anything is richer. I remember spending a weekend there. I went down from Paris on a Friday, and just got a hotel room and I stayed there until Mass on Sunday. And I made sure I saw everything in it. I walked all around the outside, all around the inside. My Old Testament imagination was so engaged by Chartres, because there's your thing about the allegorical—they read the Old Testament in constant relation to Christ, as the fulfillment. And the sculpture is just incomparably beautiful in its execution.

But then there are no better windows, and most of them are real medieval windows from the thirteenth century. Nothing sings to me more—just the way it's situated, the topography of it. You come up to Chartres, and when you go back behind it, you take the pilgrim's route up to it, and all of that; the pilgrim's journey is implicit there. But the windows look like diamonds on a black velvet background. They're like jewels, and it's the shining jewels of the New Jerusalem. So there's the anagogical sense; it's all about the journey to heaven. And then the labyrinth, which unfortunately has been kind of co-opted by a new-age spirituality. But the original labyrinth that most of the ones we see today imitate is there at Chartres.

Peterson: Yes, I know. The labyrinth is an amazing thing.

Barron: Extraordinary. I walked it several times, and it's a very powerful experience. Chartres has all of that in it and more.

Peterson: It's such a shame that these buildings . . . you see what happened in Europe, and I don't understand it, is that Europe went through this several hundred years long period of time where beauty was worshiped in a profound way, and you see that manifested in the construction of these great cathedrals that took centuries to build. The bricklayer wasn't just laying bricks. The bricklayer was building a cathedral to God—which is how our lives should be. Every little thing that we do should be imbued with that higher vision, which is possible if you have that higher vision. The contribution of that vision to Europe and to world cultures is absolutely priceless. People make pilgrimages from all over the world to view these insanely beautiful and complex buildings. And they were driven by a spirit that was hopefully unconquerable, but certainly of sufficient potency, even in a fundamentally atheistic age, to pull people in for reasons they don't even really understand—just that sheer awe at the daring of the architects.

Barron: Talk about a door or a window to the transcendent. That's a way of punching through the buffered self, those cathedrals. And don't get me started on church architecture over the last forty, fifty years, when we largely adopted a kind of brutalist modernism within Catholicism and built what Balthasar called the great "barns"—these big empty spaces. And we wonder: Why are the young people leaving in droves? The church building itself didn't sing to them in any way, which they used to do, even the imitation Gothic buildings from the 1930s. A young Catholic coming of age at that time was just surrounded by the imagery of the faith and the whole narrative of salvation.

Peterson: And the incarnation of the song in stone. You talked about part of the goal of salvation: to bring everything together, to have everything come together with a kind of integrity and in a union. Of course, music portrays that better than anything else, as far as I'm concerned. And those cathedrals were symphonies in stone. They portrayed architecturally exactly what music attempts to portray orally. And it works—it works for someone who has no belief.

Barron: Absolutely. And it's a bit of a cliché to say it, but the *Summa* of

Aquinas and the *Divine Comedy* of Dante are like that. They have that same kind of quality of integration—the whole of life being on display. And that's part of what fell apart. We needed the critique of the Enlightenment for sure. I get it; we needed that in a lot of different ways. But sadly, often that critique got overstated—the baby-bathwater phenomenon—and a lot of the integrity was compromised. How do you keep the critique without throwing out the substance? That's been one of the struggles. And much of the theology of the last couple hundred years has been so conditioned by the Enlightenment criticism. I get it, and take it in for sure, but don't so condition your theology by that critique that you lose all this stuff that we're talking about now, that has the soul-transforming power.

Peterson: It seems to me—and this is so necessary—that what's required is a re-emphasis on the potential nobility of the human being and the moral responsibility to make that nobility a reality. We don't even talk about words like that. I used the word nobility in my lectures, and it's such an archaic word. "You should have a noble goal." What child is told that now? And we're built for nobility.

Barron: You're a psychotherapist, obviously, but it seems to me that we're so concerned about people's feelings, and that the feelings getting hurt or getting repressed or something, that we're afraid that if we use that language of a noble aspiration, or "Come on, you can do better," or "You've got a serious problem," that it will awaken such negative feelings—leading eventually to self-mutilation or suicide at the limit—that we're so afraid of that that we're reluctant to use the language of nobility.

Peterson: We're afraid of hurting people's feelings in the present, and willing to absolutely sacrifice their well-being in the future. And that's the sign of a very immature and unwise culture, because the reverse should be the case. You said already: there's no up without down. And that initial conversation, when you lay things bare and you put everything out on the table, and you discuss what the problems are, and maybe the potential solutions—that's a rough conversation. It's almost more than people can bear. But if it's a discussion of reality, they're already bearing it, and at least placing it on the table indicates that there's someone who's willing to listen, and it isn't so terrible that like Voldemort it can't be named.

Barron: That's been exactly my argument, and I alluded to it earlier. You might say, "That will be too much for people to take"—but life is going to force itself on them. Life will force them into this. And then there won't be any wisdom or guide to help them with it. So if we say, "I'm so concerned about sparing people's feelings"—life doesn't care about your feelings. Nature doesn't care about your feelings.

Peterson: One of the things I learned from Jung—and I think this is a psychotherapeutic truism—is that if you're going to confront a monster, and you most certainly are, then you do it at a time and place of your choosing. Because otherwise, it waits until you're at your weakest and most vulnerable, and then it attacks. There is no monster-free pathway forward to prepare as a knight of Christ. When it comes, you're there, or in fact confronting it at its weakest point—or you cower and you wait, and it devours you. Those are your options. And we don't have the wisdom of the kind of pessimism that enables us to view life that way. We think: if we're careful and we're quiet, the monster will avoid us completely. And everyone knows that's a lie.

Barron: Sometimes when I use this language, people say, "That's great for the young men, but the young ladies don't respond to it." But years ago, my niece, who's now almost thirty, when she was about seventeen, they took her on one of these nature things, where they took the kids out into the woods, and they had to hike and they had to build their own campfire and then they had to ford streams. It's one of these really demanding things where they were up against nature and up against life. She came back utterly transformed as a human being, in a way that religion had never done. She was a Catholic all her life, gone to Mass, her uncle's a bishop. But there's nothing in our faith that changed her the way that experience clearly changed her.

Peterson: There's a serious conversation to be had with young women. A woman asked me a question on my Q&A this month. She said that her friends are really down on her because she claims to not be a feminist, but even more importantly, because she wants to have children, and they're telling her that only an evil and cruel person would bring a child into a world this terrible, and worse, to do the damage to the planet that that child will inevitably do. People are very serious about this, and they're very hard on young women.

I always think of the *Pietà*, because I think of it as the [female] equivalent of the crucifix. You have Mary there with her broken son in her arms. And I think that the great adventure for women, at least in part—this is the maternal adventure—is to bring a child into the world, knowing full well that the consequence is a crucifixion-like brokenness, and that it's still a mark of faith in the possibilities of being to participate in that and not to hide from it and to say, "Despite everything, I'm going to act out my faith in life, and in the possibilities of being, and I'm going to bring someone into the world who will be a net force for good rather than evil. And that's my moral obligation." I think to present that to young women as a major part of the adventure of their life, which is certainly the truth, is something that's attractive to far more of them than would be likely to admit it in today's time and age.

Barron: I'm glad you used the word "faith" there. Just a couple days ago, we had the feast of St. Joseph, and Joseph in the New Testament is like Abraham in the Old Testament. He's the paradigmatic person of faith. I was talking to a group of high school kids. I said, "Listen to me, everybody. I know you're going to hear this from your professors in college, and you probably hear it already, that faith means being uncritical, and you accept any old nonsense on the basis of no evidence; that it's superstition." And I said, "We're against that. And I speak now as a Catholic. Faith *and* reason.

We don't want anything subrational. Anything that is a lie and you know it, that's irresponsible; anything that's stupid and you know it, it's irresponsible to accept it. That's not faith. But what I said, which is close to what you just said, is that faith in the Bible is this willingness to risk, under the providence of God, some great adventure.

Peterson: That's exactly right. That's a great phrase.

Barron: That's what faith means in the Bible. It doesn't mean, "I'm an idiot, and just tell me any old nonsense and I'll believe it."

Peterson: No, it means that adventure. One of the things I really learned from reading the Abrahamic stories is that the fundamental call is a call to adventure, not to ease or to happiness. Even the relationship with God that's part of that adventure is wrestling with God. That's what "Israel" itself means; it's another aspect of that strange element of belief. What does it mean to believe? It means to adopt this moral burden, but it also means to wrestle with God and not to blindly accept preposterous blandishments that no one with any sense would ever swallow.

Barron: But I think we've been, again, pretty bad at propagating that. If the new atheists have gotten an awful lot of traction with that idea that religious people are just sort of naïve, superstitious, and uncritical, then we haven't explained very well what we mean by faith.

Peterson: No, we certainly haven't explained the element of it that's associated with courage.

Barron: And this is meant to happen under the guidance of a spiritual master who will help you through that and push you toward the edge and help you navigate those waters. Dante got that. All of our great spiritual teachers have it. But we've not been good at that in my judgment.

Peterson: Maybe we'll learn before it's too late. That would be nice. It was really a pleasure talking with you.

Barron: I loved it, Jordan. Thank you very much. I'm just delighted.

Peterson: More power to you as far as I'm concerned, and thank you very much for spending the time speaking with me today.

Barron: God bless you. Thanks.